the

wild mandrake

the
wild
mandrake

a memoir

jason jobin

DUNDURN
PRESS

Publisher: Kwame Scott Fraser | Acquiring editor: Julie Mannell | Editor: Susan Fitzgerald
Cover designer: Karen Alexiou
Cover image: mandrake: New York State Museum; University of the State of New York; IV bag: magicoven/shutterstock.com
Interior image: Parsons, Frances Theodora, public domain, via Wikimedia Commons

Library and Archives Canada Cataloguing in Publication

Title: The wild mandrake : a memoir / Jason Jobin.
Names: Jobin, Jason, author.
Identifiers: Canadiana (print) 20230162304 | Canadiana (ebook) 20230162339 | ISBN 9781459750746 (softcover) | ISBN 9781459750760 (EPUB) | ISBN 9781459750753 (PDF)
Subjects: LCSH: Jobin, Jason—Health | LCSH: Cancer—Patients—Biography. | LCGFT: Autobiographies.
Classification: LCC RC265.6.J62 A3 2023 | DDC 616.99/40092—dc23

We acknowledge the support of the Canada Council for the Arts and the Ontario Arts Council for our publishing program. We also acknowledge the financial support of the Government of Ontario, through the Ontario Book Publishing Tax Credit and Ontario Creates, and the Government of Canada.

Dundurn Press
1382 Queen Street East
Toronto, Ontario, Canada M4L 1C9
dundurn.com, @dundurnpress 𝕏 f ⌾

For my family

I

STAGE 2A

left neck; clavicle;
lymph node involvement;
abdomen clear

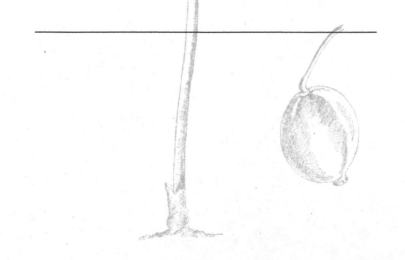

✤

AFTER TWO YEARS OF FIDDLING with the lump on my neck, and all the jokes about it being cancer, it turns out to actually be cancer. I shouldn't have said anything. There's a sense in my gut that I manifested this, that at nineteen I have developed some fell power to make the darkest comedy real. Dad and I and my younger brother and sister — the twins, Alex and Angela — are down on Vancouver Island getting together school supplies and taking a little medical vacation. My third year at the University of Victoria, and the chemotherapy will begin soon.

Dad booked us into the sketchy Island Travel Inn on Douglas. People are often having mental health crises in this patch of downtown. There are as many garbage bags as suitcases in the hands of people on the street.

While the twins watch TV, Dad takes me to the hospital for some tests. I think blood tests. I think weighing me, hopefully weighing me — the number low now, exercising very hard. I'm set up in a dark room with spotting lamps, everything else in shadow, though hospitals are meant to be well-lit — this is more a theatre or opera house.

The nurse, as she wheels in a sheet-covered steel cart, says, "The marrow test isn't a popular one."

The what test?

She peels back the sheet to reveal tools I do not recognize. It's important to recognize tools.

She goes on. "It's not everyone's favourite thing, this test."

Her eyes say more, though. They say, *Do you know about marrow? With marrow we* must *make sure.*

I'm certain there are things you don't want in marrow. When things appear in marrow the timeline can become truncated — I learned this from movies. But where do we get the marrow? Where is it from?

The doctor enters next, gloved, not making eye contact, and tells me to get into the fetal position facing the wall. He says my body will do so naturally once he begins, so I may as well get a head start.

This was described to me as a regular visit for regular tests.

Did Dad know the actual reason? He seemed not to in the cab on the way over, but now I wonder. Now that I'm in the fetal position facing the wall, I can see bristle marks in white paint. The metallic ringing of things being assembled starts up in my blind spot. I look back, and there's what could be called a needle, but it's a foot long with jackhammer-style hand grips.

The doctor notices me looking. "This will be uncomfortable. Young people have hard pelvises." Bones must soften with age, but I do not have age. "It will be fast," he says. Seconds. Insertion. Aspiration. Bone marrow is a semi-solid tissue.

The doctor numbs my skin with a regular-sized needle. Next, to ascertain the numbness, he prods the skin with a sharp spike and asks me if I feel it. I say no. He plants the giant needle's tip against my lower back — I can't tell exactly where because of the numbing, won't know until it punches through the bone that isn't numb. Am

I ready? Big push. His entire body weight on the giant needle. An animal sound leaves me. Such pressure. The needle goes through skin, then muscle, catches against my pelvis for a brief instant, then through, into my centre. I *feel* the marrow sucked out. Thickness going up the straw. I'm puddled in sweat. I think we are done. He says that I can take a few minutes to collect myself on the table before going home, and that it's probably not in the marrow, rarely in the marrow, he's sure I'll be all right.

•

I'M BACK IN YUKON FOR my first winter in years. Done the undergraduate degree now, the writing school. I miss it already. The lassitude, the slovenly lifestyle. To be back home living with my folks out in the woods is different. Before, my siblings were always there to talk with. I've never lived here like this.

The days go dark. Cold spreads through everything and forms a rime of ice on the house's windows. I sign up for a playwriting night class at Yukon College, driving the twenty kilometres twice a week through blizzards. A writer I know is teaching it — she's the mom of my little sister's best friend. Everyone here is so connected. I haven't done much playwriting, but it can't be that different, right? Just put the story into words and have the characters say them. Pretty basic.

For the class, I write a play about a genius writer named Victor with a serious head injury. They are tragic, head injuries. Will he be okay? So much on the line. And because he's a genius, it's sadder still. Will he lose the genius and be worthless and undeserving of people's love? Come find out. Everyone else in Victor's writing classes knows he's a serious artist. They are all in awe. In the world of the play, he's writing a short story about a water control officer who starts putting barbiturates and sodium thiopental — hokey truth serums — into his city's water supply in the hopes that people will, under the influence of these extremely strong drugs, love each other more. Soon, I realize that the substory of poisoning the water is more interesting than the main story about the head injury, but it's too late to change the plot.

At home, I try to smoke weed in secret and probably do not succeed. Strange having to again meet shady guys in parking lots at night. Yukon is not the same as B.C. Back on Vancouver Island, weed was always available. I'd join the orderly line out the door of the dealer's downtrodden apartment on Shelbourne, a tattooed assistant girl who was probably his wife asking what I was lining up to buy. Here, it's frozen-over parking lots, negative thirty degrees, scrambling from my car to their driver-side window. I throw in money, they hand me *something*, and I drive home, the big high-way lamps casting gold light into the car in a left-to-right swirl, like a siren spinning in its little glass cup. I'm broke, unemployed, and trying not to smoke weed but still smoking, sometimes just the black resin-goo at the bottom of the pipe, up in my childhood room, staring at the map of the world that's still on the wall, no pins on it or anything, no markers for where I'll go.

Still working on the play for class. There's a girl character now who loves Victor and visits him in hospital while machines beep and lines squiggle on monitors. They are in love. The love goes without saying and doesn't require risk or participation. They have snazzy conversations where both of them are being mean, but it's smart enough to not seem mean. One of the main themes is the concept of pareidolia, things appearing like other things — clouds that resemble dogs, trees that resemble people. As the play progresses, more and more things in Victor's life take on the likeness of other things. It's possible he's trying to tie it all together to overcome the trauma of having his skull cracked open. It's very difficult, and he struggles.

A few of my also-graduated friends are back in Yukon now, too, pursuing careers. I think they'll stay long-term, most of them. Or they leave and get pulled back. We go out to bars on weekdays and get obliterated, not everyone with jobs yet, not everyone caring yet. On nights I don't go out, I work on the play or the novel. Chipping away in the dark, as the office is right next to my parents' bedroom, Dad always yelling through the wall to be quiet. The novel is just everything I've ever known or thought, and it's kind of shit because I haven't known or thought that much. But I also think it's amazing, for the same reason.

It dawns on me that a good way to end the play would be for Victor to *mostly* rediscover his genius after the head trauma. Like, he can still be a genius. But — and this is crucial — he himself doesn't believe he gets it back. He himself doubts that the head trauma hasn't permanently damaged him, believes it has made him less of a genius, and will forever wonder what he's lost. It's not clear if the head-on collision was even his fault. When the accident happens, he's driving home from class after arguing with the girl he loves and who loves him, and then there's the crash and it's brutal and in slow motion. The argument that preceded the crash was mostly about how he was right about something having to do with writing craft — remember, he's a writing genius — and she's like, "Well, you don't have to be such an asshole about it," and he's like, "I'd rather be right than happy," and the play subtly hinting that this is a deranged thing to believe. In the end, they stay together, I think, though I never get that far. The class ends before spring, when the days are still short and the sky is white and the ground goes soft with mud that freezes each night and thaws each morning.

•

AN OLD COUPLE SITS NEAR the water fountain, close, their knees touching. Window light pools in the dishes below the woman's eyes. Her hair is the colour of ice. The man has no hair. He's dying. The thinness. Like a child's drawing of a person. She holds up a tissue, and he blows his nose. A minute later she holds up another tissue, and he blows again. And again, and again, and it doesn't stop, this ragged bleating. I don't stare. I pretend to look elsewhere. The woman holding each tissue like an orchid, with a particular fold, practised. On her lap is the kind of shallow box that holds twenty-four soda cans, and she places the used tissues inside it. Her having brought the box, knowing how it would be. The box will need to be emptied soon. Judging by the sounds that come from him, the tissues must be despoiled, but in the box they all look white.

I realize he isn't blowing his nose. A white plastic spigot juts out of his throat just below the Adam's apple. She holds each tissue over the end of the spigot, collecting. And then folds the tissue and places it in the box with the others. The box so full now it looks like the preparation for a raffle.

•

I'M ON FRANK'S COUCH IN late morning, my intestines all coiled up. We're not roommates anymore, Frank and I, but this hangover makes it feel like we are. The malaise reminds me of being in university and makes me want to go back. Grad school applications are due soon — I will do them, for sure. His folks are gone, so a bunch of people have crashed at their beautiful home overlooking the Yukon River valley. Out the window, snow-crusted spruce lean against one another. Banks of frozen fog rise from the valley basin like cotton. Ice crystals tattoo the windows. Last night, as we got drunker and drunker, the cold seemed to melt off us, and we undid jackets and took off toques and rambled through the night from one bar to the next.

There are no blinds on the ten-foot windows. Must be late with this much daylight. The moon stands out in the sky's pale blue. So many craters, how they accrue across millennia and never heal. I roll onto the floor and scramble upright. Where is my jacket? This type of cold, you always want to know where your jacket is. My wallet is in the jacket, also. I check behind the couch, the entryway, the bathroom I was throwing up in earlier. Forty below and no jacket? I don't remember getting back here — must've been a cab. I curl into a ball on the couch and drag the wool throw over my aching body and face. If I block out the sun and moon a bit longer, I'll be okay. Plotting now. A return to my car. An escape.

I sleep another hour and wake feeling like I've eaten batteries.

Mom is working at the college today, so I call to ask if I can visit. Frank drives me, lends me a thick wool pullover that itches whenever I move. It's not as warm as the jacket I can't find, but it's better than nothing.

There are few people in the college's halls as I begin to look for the nursing wing. At least it's warm. I follow signs until I see the one with my mom's name on it and enter a makeshift medical ward, still feeling dizzy and half-asleep. Eventually, I find her office by just walking down the hall. She's at her desk, working hard, like I knew she would be. Always working so hard. She gives me a look of concern, noticing that I don't have my jacket, but she doesn't ask. I explain that the jacket got stolen, that you cannot trust people in this town.

There's a mock hospital room off the hallway. With a gesture, she leads me to one of the pretend beds, says I can sleep it off. I roll into the thin quilts, burrowing, not wanting her to see me shiver. A pink mannequin stares blankly at the ceiling from the other bed.

It's studded with a million little holes where students practise inserting needles. Eventually, another nursing teacher comes in and asks how I'm doing. She has a knowing look.

"Just recently admitted," I say. "Could be anything."

"Let's check you out." She takes my vitals, hums at the right moments, wonders at my condition.

•

I'M WORKING AT MY UNCLE'S over the summer, home from university. Construction. Landscaping. Painting his giant wraparound deck. It's good work and pays enough to cover most of my coming year's rent, the rest made up by Yukon school grants. I usually work with my cousin Anna or some of her brothers. We grew up almost like siblings, always camping and fishing and going on road trips through the prairies to visit our grandparents. We're out in the sun all day. My skin browns, and freckles pop out everywhere. My hands get cut up from wood and hammers and chisels. It's summer, I'm still in full remission, and things feels durable. It's good to have some money and to work with family.

My uncle has a mining exploration company based out of his house at the southern end of town. My family lives on the northern end, forty kilometres away. The drive is long, but he pays for some of the gas, so it's not the worst.

His place is like a log cabin the size of a house, and each year he pays us to paint linseed oil into the logs so they don't crack in the winter. First, he trucks in a bunch of scaffolds from a contractor who does rentals downtown — these scaffolds are in bad shape sometimes, rotted through, split down the middle. We get good at assembling and disassembling them. Most important is having them level and not forgetting any of the cross braces. We set up the scaffold, paint for a few days, then move it clockwise, and like this we work our way around the house. I'm drenched in oil by the end of the day, the stuff in my hair, my eyes. It's tough to get linseed oil out of your eyes once it gets in. Lots of stinging and irritation. The east side of the house is on a steeper slope, which makes the roof farther from the ground. On this tall side, we set up four levels of scaffold, which is always one too many, the whole apparatus wobbling at that height. Steel sounds. Vertigo. Two of the scaffold's legs are balanced on logs. We get ropes and safety harnesses, then don't use them.

Later in the summer, we build an insulated chicken coop and hatch the chickens from eggs. The little birds in our hands, given names, so soft, soon forgetting us, or pecking the youngest chicken to death, or taken by foxes and eagles, one even riddled with cancer, bulbous and featherless, walking in circles until one day it just disappears.

At the north edge of his property are rows of storage sheds full of wasps. They haven't always been full of wasps, but this summer has been ideal for wasps. There are seven sheds in two rows, all made of old plywood and painted with the forest-green boat paint he insists we use. Some have doors; some are more open to the elements, at least in the summer. They store the tools and equipment of a small exploration business, everything a person out in the woods might ever need. The wasps are out of control. I've never seen them like this, their nests stashed among chainsaws and wall tents and pickaxes and old coolers and lumber. Nests in the rafters. In duffle bags. In torn foam mattresses. We wear insect hoods and long sleeves and work gloves. When we find a nest, we spray it with insecticidal foam, then wait, then hit it with a shovel or hammer. Sometimes the shovel blade cuts the nest in half like a coconut, the bisected cells showing each developmental stage — larva, pupa, soldier — wriggling their last moments. Otherwise, we are moving rotten lumber from the sheds into burn piles, organizing tents by whether they have enough poles, reinforcing old shelves about to collapse. Moving cinder blocks. Is all this work necessary? I don't know. Maybe not. But I know he enjoys employing people and having them work and then paying them for their work. He always shakes my hand before he gives me a cheque. And, really, that's okay.

One day, in late July, we're moving an old pile of compost from one spot to another spot. The sun flares overhead. Anna and I lean on our shovels, brows damp, taking a breath. The pile of dark-brown soil is covered with a tarp and a piece of plywood, and when I lift the half-rotted plank, mice flee in every direction. Some are babies, blind and limping in circles. Our orders are to hit any mice we see with a shovel, but we don't. Instead we give them time to escape and then drag the plywood back over the pile of almost-soil.

A few mornings later, I'm in the greenhouse enjoying the smell of plants, the humidity, when I see a mouse in the bed of tomatoes. I've got a flat piece of wood in hand, and, not thinking it through, I jab it at the mouse, hoping it will run away. Instead, I cut it in half.

Near the end of summer, we build a stone path around the back steps. The stones taken from a copper quarry out past Golden Horn and fitted together into a mosaic. I've been reading about Japanese dry gardens in one of my aunt's books. In dry Zen gardens, each stone needs its best side showing, and for each chasing stone, there should be a running-away stone. The cousins and I search the copper quarry for hours, then drive to another quarry farther down the highway. Most of the stones are sedimentary and brittle and fall apart in our hands. One quarry near Mount Sima has a deep orange canyon that people have thrown fridges and washing machines and oil drums into. Here I find a quartz boulder that I know right away is the one. It is white and crystalline, with a depression in the top that will collect rainwater for birds to drink; it's perfect and too heavy to lift. My cousin Jon and I roll the stone uphill for twenty minutes back to the truck. We get it in the box somehow, then drive back to their place with our prize.

Our work is good. We've laid a bed of white gravel in front of the house as part of our Zen idea, a riverine border that curls around the side. We've planted new birch trees in circles of chopped peat wood. There's a give and take between my uncle and aunt with my more philosophical renovations. She's interested in the Zen ideas; he wants us to avoid pouring too much water near the foundation, as he always expresses fears the house will tip over like a toy block.

Our big white stone ends up next to the wild roses near the staircase. We wedge it so that the side with the shallow basin faces the sky and will collect rain for birds, like I wanted, though the basin isn't that deep and will not collect much. But birds don't need much, and certainly less than I do. I stand at the base of the stairs on one of the last days of summer and look at the white stone, and I can't tell if it's a running-away stone or a chasing stone. I don't know who else cares about this stuff. What does it matter, one stone or another stone, chasing, being chased? It's hard to know the difference.

•

I'M STOPPED AT THE EDGE of a dense willow forest and starting to question my career in mining exploration. On the surface all you need to do is get dropped off by a helicopter and follow a straight line, stopping every so often to hammer a wooden stake into the ground. But the solitude is getting to me. The dense willows are getting to me. Willows grown so tight I can't see through them.

I've been working a grid along the Bonnet Plume River for weeks. Every 450 metres as the crow flies, I set a post and then nail in a tin plaque with the relevant serial number. Then another 450 metres, following the GPS. High summer in Yukon, and there's money to be made, though I suspect no one will ever see these or come here again. We're hundreds of kilometres north of Whitehorse by truck, another hundred by bush plane, seventy or eighty more by helicopter. Our base camp is to the south, I think. Would have to pull out the map to be sure. I've been getting confused and losing my way of late. This patch of forest identical to that one. Each morning we helicopter wherever we're working, and each night, once they find us, we fly back.

I miss the mountains. The first weeks here were all shale slopes and scree and rubble. I'm afraid of heights, and the vertigo had me this close to quitting. But I'd never live it down with my family, so I stayed, tried to build a little wall around each moment on the slopes and never look down. But now, in the swamp, I miss the mountains. Funny how that happens. Now, it's moss and long serpentine lakes that cut across the GPS lines, and mud, and bogs, and more mosquitoes than seems possible.

I'm losing it. Maybe too long out here.

Each night in camp, the other guys and I smoke weed and eat five thousand calories. They talk about their girlfriends when they're high. I don't have a girlfriend and don't really know what I talk about. We sleep early and are up at 5:30 a.m. for breakfast and to get our gear ready. The helicopter spools up around 6:15 a.m.

I've never lived in a wall tent like this. A plywood surface in each corner for a foam mattress. A table in the middle. A stove near the back wall. There are about a dozen other wall tents, the building where they store the core samples for the geologists, and the cook shack. Our little town in a valley next to the Bear River. It's very nineteenth century. Laundry machines are in a bigger framed tent in the back row, this one also with a cylindrical plastic shower stall running water pumped up from the river. The shower stall is pretty gross, my one buddy saying he goes in with garbage bags on his feet due to how much masturbating must go on. The camp has no internet, though. No television. And every evening, as the night's perpetual twilight settles in, a mouse climbs into our tent through a crack near the stove and scurries from corner to corner looking for food, then leaves through the same crack.

For ten hours each day, we're out in the woods hiking, marking trail, and either making new mining plots or chasing after old ones. With the old ones, the posts are supposed to already be in the ground at the proper GPS coordinates, but often aren't, or they've fallen off a cliff or been buried in moss or been chewed through by bears. We still hammer tin tags onto the old posts when we find them. The tags renew mineral rights and prevent another mining company from stealing them.

There are no days off. You get used to it. And on the rare times fog rolls in too thick for the helicopter, we get the day. That moment when the pilot says he can't fly is a bliss I don't think I could re-create outside these conditions. I lower myself back onto the foam mattress and close my eyes. There's gentle rain against the canvas and my knees ache and the skin is rubbed off my shoulders from the pack straps, and it feels so good.

But now I'm at these willows. I don't want to go into the willows, but there's no way around. I linger at the edge all the same, drinking water, pacing. I must follow the GPS line. That is my job. To navigate around? Maybe. But the posts I need are in the willows somewhere, based on the coordinates. I need to find those old posts and hammer a new serial number onto each one with the butt of my axe and then nail them together and wrap them with red flagging so that at some point in the future, if another person comes this way, they will see them and know.

No choice but to go. I get out my axe and push into the trees. To move forward is like doing tai chi. Branches hem me in. Tree sap everywhere. Line of sight only a few feet. As I walk deeper in, emerald bugs cascade onto me from above. The more branches I knock aside and move through, the more bugs fall. I need a machete but don't have one. I use my weight and rip branches down, fold the thinner trunks in two. Each step a contortion. Recently I've been talking to myself a lot in French-accented English. Doing this now. *Allo. Bonjour. I ham walking trew da wood.* I don't know why. One of the guys on the crew is a Quebecer and, well, *I am too*, from my father's side, but that's no reason for this talking to myself. This going insane. Long conversations. I tear branches and kick stumps, ears piqued for every vague sound as I lunge ahead. So long out here in the woods, you start listening, hearing. Any new sound an alarm. Yesterday, as I sat in the moss eating my sandwich and listening, a vole scurried toward me until it was almost in my lap. I must be an oddity out here. The new creature.

The willows go forever. No end to them or gradient of light. After a kilometre I'm losing it, claustrophobic, yelling, in a half run. Bars of sun filter down through the leaves, the light full of pollen. Everything is green and flexible, swaying in a wind that smells like silt. Where are the posts? There is no trail, no flagging tied to branches. No chance at the posts. I've accepted it. Gone forever. Now swinging the axe, finding space, anything for a different biome, sap everywhere, the trees cloistered and raining emerald bugs into my hair, my chin, the corner of my eye.

And then I'm through, back to spruce trees, panting, my shirt soaked. I can't hear the river yet, not with my ears, but I also *can* hear it and know it's close. The ground starts to slope in the way ground dips toward water. Then the wet hiss. The roar. Brighter bands through the trees, movement. The Bonnet Plume. I break from tree cover and see the river in full, what we've snuck around for weeks. A fast one. The sound of it on the air. Too deep to ford. Grey stones gird the shore, their sides covered in slime. I squat at the river's edge and trail my fingers through yellow froth. I splash the sweat off my face, the water so cold, fed by glaciers. With some heavy stones, I build a berm in the shallows and put my last box of

grape juice in. I then sit on a piece of driftwood and go back to listening. The water is so loud, I can't hear much beyond it. But other
noises come. Sounds from the trees. Birdsong. My pulse. Breath.
Carabiners hanging off my pack rattled by the wind. Such a chorus.
And when I'm gone, so will they be gone, and we won't remember
one another, as it was in the beginning.

•

AFTER EVERY WRITING WORKSHOP, INSTEAD of going to the
film class we're all registered in, some friends and I go to a bar near
campus called Maude Hunter's. We used to be like, "Should we skip
the film class?" but now we don't even mention it. There's nothing
wrong with the class or the professor — we just do not go. Maude's
is an old coach house–type pub built of dark, glossy wood. The place
is kind of crummy, and there's the occasional mouse underfoot, but
it's close enough to walk, and Wednesdays are wing night.

While drinking too fast, we writing students accumulate a grotesque mountain of wing bones. Our conversation mostly about
writing and all the things that make us mad. After getting wasted
enough that we should leave the bar so as not to spend any more
money, we walk to the house of the one friend who lives nearby. The
walk fresh out of the bar is always the best walk. I'm no longer cold
or hot, my body temperature more a sound, more a vibration. And
the relaxation, the softness of drunk muscle.

We walk through the lamp-lined streets from one globe of light
to the next, the rain a golden mist through these lamps' conical
auras. The friend's house is often dark, looking abandoned. There's
a roommate there when we arrive. Always the same roommate:
ghostly, in pyjamas, barefoot, says "Hi" when we come in. The vibe
being that this roommate has done lots of hallucinogens and is now
very nice and darkness-loving.

We walk upstairs to the couch area and settle in. There is lots of clutter in the house, but it's not exactly dirty, not exactly clean. Just lots of stuff. I never know where things should go or where things are. We all drink more, and some of my friends take big bong rips. I can't do bong rips after drinking alcohol — makes me puke every time. So, even though I truly love bong rips and take them every waking moment when I'm not drunk, I do not take bong rips at this guy's place.

Then we talk more about writing and usually complain about the annoying guy in the workshop who writes insensitive comments and thinks himself a genius. This guy is using the term *Murakami* a lot, and I don't know what it means. Two of the friends are dating, and the girl is always so sleepy once we get on those couches. She falls asleep right away after getting stoned and naps right there, making little sigh noises. No matter how loud we talk or argue, she does not wake up. We keep on playing, maybe card games, maybe board games — Bananagrams, Scrabble. And it's so dark in the house, I can't see shit. Salt lamps and Christmas lights decorate the borders of the room. Against one wall is a shelf of alphabetically organized DVDs and books and graphic novels and comics. But it's fun, though I don't like how far this place is from my place, and getting home is annoying once the beer energy goes away.

Sometimes one of the girls drives me back to my place. I think she's probably into me, because she drives me and sits there next to me in the car, making eye contact, waiting for me to do something. I sit there not doing it. Since the cancer, I've been so unable to do this shit, even though I'm lonely. After some moments pass, I crack the door and thank her for the ride. She's probably too drunk to be driving. We repeat this pattern several times. The pattern of going to the guy's place. The pattern of getting offered the ride. The pattern of our group getting wasted and being separate from the other little groups out getting wasted and talking about how our writing comments are insensitive. I try really hard to be kind in my comments, but I don't know what I'm doing. I hope they're okay. I hope we're all okay.

•

DURING SCHOOL, I NEVER PLAN stories. There are characters, and things happen to them — *bad things* — but the events have no causality. Sometimes bad events occur for no reason, is all. Why can't stories have that? There is no rule against bad things happening to characters beyond their most fervent wish for control.

The truth is, once a narrative allows cause and effect to infiltrate it, readers want resolution. Better to let the bad events have no particular cause or possible solution. A man is maimed by a falling tree. A spouse cheats even though the relationship is fine. This type of stuff. Car accidents, too. A good car accident can work wonders.

Most of my early stories, the ones from school, are about misunderstood, sad men. Weird men. Men with redeeming qualities, who mean well but have done something horrible, either on purpose or by accident. Men who are often in the woods. Men who masturbate and feel wronged and watch birds fly through the air. All these men smart enough to know what the men in these early stories may represent or be. But can they know the meaning of themselves? No. Impossible.

Stop writing these men. Instead, write protagonists who are women. Yes. Brilliant. These women can be loners, like falconers or huntresses, who live in the woods and enjoy nature but are maybe also prone to sex thoughts, and, yeah, also misunderstood, a little misunderstood. Maybe lonely. Maybe women who have done or are about to do something horrible. You just want to forgive them so much. Such cool women. Love these women. So exciting. Will they make it? Will they overcome? Spend nights until 4:00 a.m.

wondering how they can make it in the story, how they can win. They never make it.

The stories often have no real plot and instead just the weirdness, the sex, the having done something horrible. And in workshop, when it's my turn, everyone nods and opens their eyes a bit wider and says things like *So original. Strange! Unique. What's going on here?* Everyone nods. Everyone agrees. *What exactly is going on with the guy in the woods? Did he masturbate right after getting maimed? No, no, it was simultaneous with the maiming. So weird. Do they have sex? Is there sex here? It's subtle. Never can be sure.* Love these conversations. Do more. Always have birds. Never give up on birds.

I take the comments home, put them in a giant stack next to my dresser and sometimes go over the good ones, the ones with really clear and easy-to-read handwriting and feedback that is mostly positive, not just checkmarks to denote goodness. Actual phrases of goodness are important. Actual *I couldn't get this guy getting maimed out of my head, but has he done something horrible?*–type comments in the margins, in blue ink, cursive. Read over those comments and think how much they mean to me, how this person went through the process of writing them down like they would be stacked just so and stained by soup and held in an ever-growing pile on the carpet until the silverfish start to eat the pages and I toss them in a Dumpster and wish they'd been emailed.

Near the end of term, I write a story about a car accident. In the story, a man awaits trial for striking and killing a teenager with his car. While locked up, he writes letters to the kid's parents — an epistolary element helps me pretend the accident was real. And the thing I'm trying to get at through the letters is that the guy isn't sure whether he swerved on purpose. There is no bad-blood history between the man and the now-dead teenager, let me be clear. He had no reason for doing such a monstrous thing. But he just *isn't sure* that the collision wasn't in some way intentional. The parents aren't too keen on the man's letters, you can bet. They aren't the main characters, though, so he keeps writing them. Mostly, the story focuses on the man's past, but that reveals no clear reason why he might try to hit someone with his car. So he's going around and around in his mind about whether he did or whether he didn't, and he starts feeling crazy. Then he gets convicted and the story is over.

But as the classes end and new classes begin, I start reading George Saunders, and it blows my mind to see plots. I begin to write plots. At first, they don't make sense, and people in the class write in the margins that they don't understand why so-and-so is taking a given action. I crumple these feedback letters and let them fall behind my dresser, where the spiders live. What does it matter why a character is doing an action? The action should be explanation enough. So I start to think about it even more: action is when the character does something. Seeing action, the reader seeks to know *why* the character does it. We all want our schema of who a person is to align with the actions they take. Otherwise we are stupid and not paying attention. What about the people I know: my brother, my sisters, my father, my mother? When they act, do I know why?

When my father would come into the house, when I was young, and declare that he had brought candy or soda or some treat with him, and we'd all rush over, and then he'd say that he didn't actually have the promised treat and it was a joke, did I understand why he did that? Deep down, I assumed the fake-candy thing was something *his* father had done when entering their house all those years before, this father of my father dying of a brain tumour when my dad was a teenager. So why did my grandfather pretend to have treats, if he did, in fact, pretend to have them? They didn't have much money, for one. The joy of even pretend candy might have seemed worthwhile. But even that isn't an explanation. There is an action with no clear and obvious causality behind it, yet that actor with the fake candy is *a person*. I should have asked, could still ask. Could call and say, "Dad, what was the deal with the pretend candy? Why did you do that when you came home?" And he might answer, though I doubt it. More than likely, he'd not remember, or say he was just having fun, which he was, and then he'd wonder for one whole minute why I'd ask such a question twenty-five years later, and he'd not really get it. We've never really understood one another. Maybe two characters cannot always communicate.

•

AFTER A FEW MINUTES OF waiting in a yellow hall, a nurse with tired eyes comes for me. When doctors want to know if cancer treatment is working, they give you a PET scan; it's like a CT scan, but more radioactive, equal to about 250 chest X-rays. Not ideal. But it's only one — my second one, yes, but hopefully my last. PET machines are also rarer and more expensive than CT scanners, so I need to travel to Vancouver.

She leads me to the patient intake room, where I'm told to go behind a curtain and take off my clothes and get into a hospital gown. She settles me, now robed, into a cushioned recliner and sets up an IV. No matter what happens to me in the hospital, there is always an IV. I've learned this. The sting of the catheter entering the vein takes my mind off whether I'll be late for my flight back to the island. I'm only here for the day. She flushes cold saline into the IV, which burns. Then she's gone to get her armour on, which takes about fifteen minutes in my experience.

She returns wearing a lead apron and lead gloves, pushing a cart with a lead crucible on it. Crucibles are one of those things that, even if you do not know the word for it, seeing one places that word in your mouth. She drapes a lead bib over my penis area. From the crucible, she withdraws an injector of nuclear glucose, then fixes it into the IV's in valve. Am I ready? Yes, do it. In goes the magic sugar, its metallic taste on my tongue. She says I'll need to sit here for an hour. To marinate. The sugar will move through my body and settle into the areas of greatest metabolic activity. Cancer loves this sugar and will drink it all up. On the scan results, cancer will glow brighter than areas without cancer, will shine with rainbow colours, or so I imagine. Maybe the scan results are drab and incomprehensible, not even resembling a body. Maybe they are a black-and-white diagram of my abbreviated future.

I sit in my gown, irradiated, and wait. There isn't a clock in the room. Bleach soaks the air. The floor is a beige-and-brown-speckled camouflage.

The hour elapses and they take me to the scanning room. There are the typical radioactive signs on the walls, the big doughnut machine with the plank you lie on, the essentials. The technicians don't waste any time. I get arranged on the steel plank. They drape a warmed wool blanket over me. Into the doughnut goes the plank. Whirring, groans, clanks. I'm asked to breathe; I'm asked to not breathe. Then we are done, and they know what they need to know. It's so hard not to simply ask them. They are the technicians, after all; they have computers and screens in their thick-windowed room and *must know*. Right? Am I being crazy? They fucking must know. Can't they see the scan as it happens? Can't they see the glow of devoured sugar in lungs and breasts and brains and pancreases? How many patients come through here and lie on the plank and listen to the whirrs, and the technicians are in their shielded room looking at the screen and knowing that that person is dead? The person all hopeful, but the technicians knowing. They can't say anything, as they are not radiologists, but I'm convinced they can see. Or perhaps there is a system in place to prevent any visual representation of the scan from appearing on their monitors. To save them the emotional harm of knowing. Maybe for the best. But I so want to ask as they pluck the IV from my arm, want to say "How does it look?" Even if they didn't answer, there'd be something. Reassurance. Pity. The subtle look to the side of a liar.

As I leave the nuclear medicine wing, they give me an envelope. They say I may need this for my flight if my body triggers the radiation detectors at the airport. This is a post-9/11 thing, these detectors. How radioactive am I? I read the letter, and it says I shouldn't be near a pregnant woman for the next twenty-four hours. Okay. What about on the plane? What do I say? Do I say "Can I move seats?" But why do I want to move seats? Can I please specify? No, maybe not. Just say "I don't feel well, I'm dizzy, I need an aisle, or a window. I need to be alone."

•

TREVOR HAS DRIVEN THE THREE of us other crew members to a swamp in the middle of the bush. We're done for the day, the sun's out, and we are going to see if the Argonaut floats. This test is not part of the mining exploration and will not locate any gold or uranium. "It's supposed to be amphibious," he says about the Argonaut. Amphibious. Up to now we've only driven the eight-wheeled machine down a mud trail to get to our daily job site, where we cut lines through the forest so that geologists can walk around looking for metal. A few times we've run the machine into a tree on purpose. Just running into the tree, slow-like, and the tree bends, then snaps, and we drive over it. I don't know why we do this. It's not clear.

We're based out of Beaver Creek, a tiny town near the Yukon-Alaska border. For this first week, we have no helicopter and instead take a four-wheeler and the Argonaut down a flooded trail to the work grid. As more of the trail gets submerged, we're forced into bigger and bigger detours with the four-wheeler, as it is not even somewhat amphibious. I've always been more a snowmobile guy, so someone else drives the four-wheeler, too fast and swerving, and I'm on the back with my hands wound through bungee cords we've strapped across the gear rack — I would be safer holding on to the driver, but that's not happening.

We're staying at an old two-floor motel in town. My bed's caved in down the middle. What these rooms have seen. I'm too young to notice or think about the shape of the place, but it's there at the back of my mind like a shadow. My cousin, Benji, shares the room with me. He somehow smuggled a giant jug of Crown Royal here in his pack. He's still in high school. A couple other guys on the crew are older, some really old, fifties maybe. Once they find out about the Crown Royal, they come visit our room more. They poke their head in to say hi, but it's to drink the Crown Royal. How they manage to hike all day after what they do to themselves at night, I don't understand. Able to hike ten hours without stopping, puking the whole way, with almost no food. One of them barges into our room multiple times at 3:00 a.m. to use our bathroom. I don't know why. But it wakes me up, and I hear him in the dark. He's drunk, and smashing around. I guess we don't lock the door or there is no lock or locking it doesn't occur to me. I wake up and lie with my eyes closed to the suddenly on bathroom light as the guy does his thing. Then he bangs out of the room, and I go back to sleep.

Trevor has the Argonaut right at the edge of the swamp. We're on the mossy bank, scoping out the scene. I've got my arms crossed. We all have our arms crossed as we decide if the machine is, in fact, amphibious. Do we see any cracks in the main body? Do we see any evidence that it floats? The body looks to be hollow. And the wheels — eight wheels is a lot, is plenty — they must be hollow too, logically. The thing's low to the ground, army green, two seats up front, a bench in the back. The Argonaut can turn in place, though

I can't figure out how. There's a winch on the front, which we've used to pull down trees too big to drive over.

Trevor hops in the front passenger seat; I get in the back. François wants to drive, as always. He's this old French chef and mining guy, owned a restaurant maybe, is verbose when criticizing our motel restaurant's food — the chef fired yesterday for coming out drunk, having cut himself without realizing, blood on the plates.

François nudges the Argonaut forward and we drop off the bank with a hollow splash. Bobbing there. We are heavy. Low now. Water laps at my boots. By spinning the wheels, we move across the pond at a crawl. Eventually I ask to be let back onto shore, and I stand on the moss watching François trundle the Argonaut back and forth in the water, a cigarette drooping from his lips, one hand on his belly. We are now amphibious. I soon sit on a patch of moss and eat beef jerky from my pack as they play in the water. It might sink, is my thinking.

Folks are always designing machines that *can* do something, just barely, and they think this makes the machines important. Why not do it well? Why not specialize? Or maybe that's what I should cling to. The potential to scrape by. What greater machine is there than the body, in spite of its countless flaws? My body *can* survive. Even if it wasn't designed to. So I sit on the moss watching the Argonaut in its slow arc across the pond, how it vibrates and wobbles, and understand why it matters, understand making sure it can float, even if it will not be remembered, even though we'll never come back here.

•

WE ROOMMATES HAVE GATHERED IN the basement along three mismatched tables to eat. This is my first Thanksgiving with friends. We are all twenty. There are no responsible adults. My body thrums with the need to hold on to the image of us around the table. If I die, I want to have a clear image. I'm two weeks into a chemo cycle and almost back to baseline. The weakness lingers. My hair's going, but I've buzzed it short so none of the roommates will notice. Otherwise, I'm just very cold all the time, often shivering or needing sweaters, my blood counts low still. I'm young and resilient. Bouncing back.

Six of us Yukoners live here, studying at the University of Victoria. The rent is $350 each, and when we need to pay it, I walk down to the gas station, withdraw the cash, and add my portion to the thick envelope we hand to the landlord, who might not speak English but does know the correct amount of money when she sees it. There's the feeling, sitting at this table, that we won't all be living together next year, and it's always at the back of my mind. These things end; that is the point of them. Better to freeze time now and binge drink here forever.

I've known all the roommates for years. They are good to me.

We've invited a few friends to the dinner, mostly Yukoners, though some locals, a girl one of my roommates is in love with, other people from school, a poet, a soccer player. Everyone's getting wasted, except the one religious guy and the roommate who has been becoming religious right under our noses. Good for him. He should pursue joy where he finds it.

Several people eat weed brownies before the meal. I pass, skittish about dosage. I'm sipping wine from a blue plastic kid's cup. I haven't made any food tonight, though it's a potluck and everyone else *has*. My having cancer somehow makes it not rude. Cancer gets you out of many responsibilities and, being young, I still think that's a good thing.

The girls live upstairs; the boys live downstairs. Three and three. The girls make the turkey. I don't know how to cook anything, or really take care of myself. For the chemos, Mom's been coming down and getting a hotel room that I go to for the initial bad days so I don't have to be around my roommates and partying and all that. I don't want them to see me during the bad days, anyway; must maintain the illusion. The doctors have me on ABVD chemotherapy — a very normal regime, old school, draconian.

Tyler, a visiting friend, is getting wasted. Allison, one of the upstairs roommates, is getting wasted. Raph, another visiting Yukoner, is on the weed brownies, but also getting wasted. I really want to drink until I can't see or remember, but don't have it in me. Still too fragile, especially my stomach. The death taste in my mouth hasn't gone away yet.

I drink my wine with both hands on the cup and start to feel it after only a few sips.

It's my birthday. It's always my birthday around Thanksgiving. They sing, and I don't know whether to sing along or just blush and be embarrassed. I do both.

I'm doing one writing class this term. Reduced course load, no other way. The one class is plenty with the treatments going on. Chemo has me feeling extremely selfish, and even the three-hour workshop once a week is an infringement on whatever it is I think is owed to me in terms of leisure time. The class is mixed genre with a visiting professor, Seán Virgo. He's cultured-seeming, foreign in some way, and chain smokes during the workshop's five-minute break. Must have been smoking for decades, by the sound of his voice. He's the kind of old smoker poetic-type who seems indestructible. As it's mixed genre, the workshop itself consists only of students who didn't get into the classes they wanted. Wannabe novelists and poets and dramatists and television writers. The feedback is sour. Arguments break out during most classes. No one gets along, really. There's this pretty fencer who is the only good writer, and she makes me realize that people can actually be good writers while they are young.

All I think about is dying and being buried in soil. Doom is on me. Not telling the other students about the cancer makes me feel important. But it's nice to show up to the building, to see people, to be in a cohort. I write a lot in the slots between treatments when I'm well enough. Won't these other students be surprised when I die suddenly and the work I submitted to *their* class becomes anthologized everywhere posthumously and they are enshrined into history.

Early in the term, I meet with Seán and tell him about my situation, and he is much less demolished than I want him to be. There's the sense he's seen things I don't yet understand. I'm still wallowing in loss and not able to see the world from any solid vantage. He's in his sixties, maybe older. Our mortality is different and arrived at differently; this difference girds the corner of his wrinkled eye and is a comfort when he talks to me.

From the very first infusion, the chemo goes bad. Right as the nurse sticks the IV in the vein on top of my hand, the room becomes a chessboard of black and white squares, and I faint. The only time it's ever happened. After that, we don't do any more hand IVs. I make it through that first treatment and spend the next few days on the couch at Mom's hotel. It's like a fever dream. She's in full nurse mode, which makes me feel bad. Helpful and selfless like she's always been — the packing us lunches we traded off for candy, the cleaning, the driving hundreds of kilometres a day so we all got to soccer and dance and skiing and math tutoring and everything. It's too much to hold in my head.

I sleep on the couch and watch hotel cable where detectives catch an endless stream of rapists and murderers with colourful backstories. Mom brings me digestible foods: toast, eggs, pasta and cheese, apples. I'm a total fucking baby and miserable. Tossing all night, covered in sweat, and trying to choke nausea pills and steroids down every morning. Just watching television and not going outside. Just being an asshole. No exercise or sunlight. This is not the way to do chemo, but I don't know that yet.

After the drugs leave my body enough for me to smile, I take a cab back to the Yukon house — we call it the Crack Shack, though it's not that bad. It's good to be back in my own bed.

The infusions come every three weeks, so I get about ten days of decent life and ten days of misery in a rotation. The first days that I start feeling okay during the first and second cycles cause a mega-contrast high. I am flying. Back to the joy of being twenty and living in a house with my friends. Is this what I've been taking for granted? But the contrast soon fades, and I forget about it.

Whoever made the turkey did a good job. Some of the other dishes have burnt bits here and there, but it's all tasty, all made with love. I drink more wine. We are laughing, eyes with that couple-drinks shine, cheeks reddened. We are capable of anything. Soon, one of the girls is licking whipped cream off a guy's nipple. The weed-brownie people are getting weird as they mix it up with booze. I eat little helpings and a tiny piece of pumpkin pie, trying to take it slow.

The whole basement is a mess. The soccer player who doesn't know us well is getting a bit traumatized. Our roommate who invited the soccer player will soon become a born-again Christian, but we don't know that yet. Later, I wonder if our generally slovenly basement and substance abuse drove him to it. Frank and I aren't exactly the best roommates. Both of us disorganized, not into cleaning, me always listening to loud rap music and smoking weed and bringing other people there to smoke weed. Sometimes getting so stoned I'll put on a pot of soup and leave it on the burner, max heat, for hours until the entire house billows with smoke and it takes weeks for the smell to leave. Amazing there are no fires. No major injuries. Even when my roommate Aislinn falls off the top floor's stair railing on Halloween, twelve feet to the basement, she just rolls out unscathed. We are truly blessed.

•

FRANK AND I ARE IN the basement of the Crack Shack, watching *CSI: Miami* on the big green couch, when we see a crane fly. These are the things that look like giant mosquitoes but don't drink blood and are just annoying and clumsy. I swat the crane fly from the air. Hard to miss it. It tumbles onto the carpet between the couch and the wall-mounted electrical heater. It's dark in the basement, because we are very high and want it to be dark, but I can still see the corner where the crane fly fell. Frank and I lean over the couch arm to check if it's truly dead or just faking. From behind the heater there emerges a leg, then another leg. We recoil. A giant spider dashes out, puts the struggling crane fly on its back, and returns to its hiding spot.

First, we confirm that we just saw what we think we saw. The stories match. It'd be better if it was a hallucination. We then go looking for a screwdriver, because there are limits. The kitchen's miscellaneous drawer of things is filled with stuff like straws, bags, birthday hats, and a can opener. No screwdriver. Does the heating bracket even come off the wall? Must be connected to the electrical, which in this old piece-of-shit house is probably a death trap, so perhaps we shouldn't be tampering with it to get at a spider. After some deliberation, we grab a bottle of Febreze and spray the laundry-scented mist into the crack where the spider went, trying to drive it out or get it wet or poison it.

The spider does not come out.

All out of ideas, I go to the fridge for an apple. The apples are not in the crisper but on the shelf above. The fridge. Our fridge situation has been getting more and more dire in recent weeks. At some point, there was a leak in our bad fridge. The landlord may have been told about the leak or may not have been told. Our fridge sees a lot of activity — beer coming out, beer going in, beer coming back out — so stuff falls down into the area below the crisper drawers. Normally the grossness of fallen debris in a fridge would have its limits — much like spider size has limits — but with how wet everything is in there, the issues compound. At first, I'd notice regular stuff floating in the water, ginger or mushrooms or garlic skin or cheese or juice or whatever. But eventually it formed a puree, thicker and darker each week. I don't want to clean it, because it's not *my* fault, and Frank and Harry don't want to clean it either, because it's not *their* fault, so no one cleans it. Cleaning the fridge now is so far out of the question, I can't even imagine it.

I don't like being this stoned and having to stare down at whatever has grown at the bottom of the fridge. Call it sludge. Call it a bog. I'm being unfair. It's not like we *never* clean. We're pretty good about everything other than the fridge. If you forget the fridge, and sort of the bathroom, then it's not that bad.

I get my apple from the shelf and check it for bruises. This apple looks good. I wash it to make sure it's nice and clean and go back to the couch. The way you move from scene to scene when stoned. Now teleported back into the struggle against the spider. I'm careful sitting down, don't want any more bruises. We got the old green couch for free when we moved in — it smelled like cat piss, and the cushioning had partially detached from the arms. The arms are now sharp blocks of wood that I keep smashing my hip against. At least the cat-piss smell seems to have lessened after ten months, though it could be acclimation.

Frank is back watching *CSI: Miami*, and I slide carefully onto my portion of the couch and watch too. These rapists can't be stopped. Or can they? I try not to think about the spider. We'll have to deal with it at some point. That one is too big. Can't be lived with. This basement always has us dropping cups onto spiders and asking the girls to come downstairs to see. They gasp, and we gasp, and then we all stand around delaying the part where we somehow remove the cup. The silverfish are worse than the spiders, anyway. A silverfish that attacked me in the bathroom must've been a century old, five times bigger than any I'd ever seen in my life, inches long. But silverfish eat dust and paper and walls, and will outlast us. So many creatures here. Sometimes a black cat comes to my window and stares at me while I'm working at my computer. I won't notice it until the *meow* shocks me from whatever revery I'm in, and there it will be, watching. I don't let the cat in, too allergic, but it still sits there, the window right at the height of the concrete walk that goes from the street to our backyard. The cat wants food, I imagine. Or to be let in and held. Or something else more complex than that, if there is such a thing.

•

I'M ON BEER FOUR — the only good beer — when we decide to go boating. Three buddies and I are at the lake to camp for the night. I know we shouldn't go boating, but also that we will. My dad's left his old sawed-off freighter canoe tied to a willow on the rocky shore. We grab our beers and walk across the grass to a little path that goes down to the water. The lake is a gold mirror. What an evening. The boat is painted royal blue this season, its sides pitted and shiny with fibreglass. As we jostle the boat while hopping in, spiders swarm out from nooks and scatter. I'm in charge of the motor, taking some time to remember how it works. Two buddies push us out with the oars. I figure out the choke eventually and start the little outboard with a couple pulls. It makes a ragged whine. I sit on a milk crate. We've all got seats after a fashion: there's the crossbar at the tip of the boat, behind that a plywood bench, and at the back a pew my family rescued from the old burnt-down church.

I show them the special fishing spot on the other side of the lake, though we didn't bring any rods. You always take your buddies to the special fishing spot if you trust them. I round the point on the far shore and slow down, the motor at a low hiccup. I always know the spot because the water is clear and deep and has long, tendril-like plants that reach up from the depths. You can't see the bottom of the lake, only the top of the plants; it's terrifying. I don't swim in the fishing spot. We never catch much here nowadays, not trout anyway, but it will always be the spot. Maybe too much fishing, or the trout went deep, or who knows. We could go back and get rods, but we won't. This is a joy ride. This is drinking beer and opening the throttle as mosquitoes hit your cheek.

The air is nice on the water. Plant smell off the wetlands. Loons warble in the distance and dive whenever we get close. We can't go as fast as we want to with such a small motor, but we try all the same, throttle all the way around, waves cresting off each side of the boat. Soon, the beer runs out and we cruise back to the property, talking about how, later, when it's perfect, we'll go out on the water *for real*.

The day's still hot. We sit on the grass with our beers, talking about university and work and girls. We kick the soccer ball around, then go and stare into the fire's coals. Even the mosquitoes look drunk. We build up the fire, then let it settle into embers for our steaks. One guy suggests we fight. Or not. I don't know. Did someone suggest fighting? Anyway, I'm wrestling the drunkest guy, and I pin him, and there's this switch that flips on — he starts to thrash. It's scary. And now I don't want to release the pin for fear of what he'll do to me, so he thrashes even harder. I can't hold him anymore. He twists and throws me to the side. I roll in a somersault, my neck diagonal. Then we're just sitting on the grass, panting, everyone aware it went too far. I stand and dust off my pants, rub the dirt off my elbows. Why are we fighting? My neck hurts even through the beer, strained maybe, twisted too far. Drunk buddy is still mad, and it's not a big deal how drunk he is, not yet. The sun's high overhead, panting too.

We eat bloody steak and drink more and sit on old camping chairs as the bugs massacre us. Sweat shines off our brows.

Hours later, the daylight is syrup. Our backs are way down in the chairs. White mountain tips stand out to the north. My dad's trapline is over there. I haven't been in years, though he asks me to come. We are sitting with our beers, full of food, swatting bugs. There's a moment of quiet where we all realize that *now* is the time to go out on the lake again. Someone says it, and we all agree. Now is perfect. No cool buzz anymore. Drunk for real. Sloppy. The fight forgotten. Again, we pull that start cord on the little motor and peel the freighter out into the navy-blue water speckled yellow with pollen. I'm not sure about life jackets. Maybe not. The water is silver where the sun hits it, the steep reflection like a great jewelled Christmas tree. No wind anymore, just calm, the surface of the lake looking curved. About a mile across, the fight buddy says it's hot, he wants to swim. Okay, man. Go swimming. He puts on a life jacket, which I guess we did bring, and leaps over the side. Big splash. We're all wet now and laughing. He goes under, pops back to the surface, cold shock. He's trembling but afloat. I know the feeling. It's like being struck, someone standing on you. All laughing still — him freezing, us warm. Fuck, it's funny. When it's no longer funny, we hoist him back into the boat, water going everywhere, and I steer us to shore.

We head back to shore. Again sitting around the fire with our beers. The firewood got wet at some point and smoke peels off in a great curtain. Blackflies cloud and draw blood behind our ears. We're moving our chairs to dodge the smoke, getting up, sitting down, always on the go. My eyes hurt. Smoke requires a careful hand. You have to think like the smoke and feel the wind on your finger. One after the other, we shift around the damp fire, lawn chair in one hand, beer in the other, and choose a new spot that we were sitting in ten minutes ago, back and forth and around, but never quite far enough, never where it feels right.

•

IN TENTH GRADE, I GET hired at a gas station with a referral from a friend. Eight twenty-five an hour. I'm told there are no raises. Attached to the station is a big concrete mechanic shop, the interior plastered with pin-up girls and pictures of old Mustangs and Firebirds. There are three car bays with lifts, almost always full, the air a mix of oil and borax and orange degreasing scrub. For a first job, not so bad. I don't even know what cancer is.

The mechanics smoke cigars while they work, talking around them, wiping their chests with old rags. One drives a mint forest-green '65 Camaro, the other a black '87 Cadillac with red leather seats the size of a double bed. We are told not to touch their cars, but they often leave them parked in the shop overnight, unlocked, so we sit in them and pretend to be driving, eyes ahead, defiant.

My buddies are all in tenth or eleventh grade, working after-school shifts and weekends, bridging the lifer who works the register during the day and the guys who do the twelve-hour shifts at night.

These night guys. The first one looks like a body found in a river. Big round eyes, cute red lunch kit in hand when he comes in, never says much. No idea what he does all night. Maybe a hidden guitar, writing sonatas. I imagine him with a pile of dominoes, not even playing, just handling them, whispering to himself.

Drug dealers come through during the day, or people who appear to be drug dealers. One guy, wearing diamonds, is there almost every week, friendly with the bosses, his car a real lemon — '90s Impala with big silver wheels, dropped low.

The night guys even have to clean the bathroom. Makes no sense. Every other job, kids clean the bathroom. Not here. The night guys are responsible. Maybe that does something to them. One time I go take a piss and the walls are streaked with blood and shit. I turn around and leave and don't tell anyone.

I don't know what happens to the first guy, but a second night guy soon replaces him. The new guy always shows up in a long black jacket, with a black lunch kit. Real mustelid vibes. Late thirties. He talks my ear off every shift as we clean and sweep and do the cash as I get ready to go home. Pink Floyd's "Money" plays whenever we do this, the radio blaring that song in particular. This guy goes on about his wife or girlfriend — it isn't clear which — and about fucking her and how she's a bitch and very demanding. I nod like I have similar problems. When girls from my school come in, I sell them cigarettes without carding, and they smile, and I feel cool. I'm Cool Guy now. I'm Guy with Cigarettes. And when these girls leave, the bosses and mechanics make comments, like us young guys better watch out, or wait our turn, or be chasing them or hunting them. It's not exactly clear what these forty-year-olds are talking about, but it also is. One girl in particular is so thin — bulimic, if what I hear at school is accurate — and right after she walks out, black-coat guy says how he'd eat her pussy for an hour, two hours, how her entire ass can fit in his palm.

The winter comes and we are full service, so I'm out in the cold pumping gas. My toenail has been growing into the side of my toe. Inflamed all day. Leaking pus. It goes on for weeks until I see a doctor, who advises removal. The surgery is pretty fast: a needle injecting what feels like liquid fire into the toe, headphones playing jazz, then the sense of someone pulling very hard. After that, I'm limping around outside in negative forty, one foot in a sneaker, the other in my mom's old leather Birkenstock with two wool socks, asking customers if they want a fill-up.

I like to buy lotto tickets when working. Being the person selling them puts me in a position to do this while underage. I stack five scratch-and-wins so that on the camera it looks like I'm only holding one. I pay for one and cash any prizes to myself. I am very smart. The bosses don't do inventory or watch the CCTV, as far as we know. They must not, because I never hear about it. Winning ten or twenty bucks a shift takes the edge off and makes me feel valued. But I don't win that often, and it makes me sad to see all the people coming in with a damp light in their eyes, buying ten, twenty, thirty tickets, spending hundreds of dollars, like this will be the day.

Some of the other guys keep a casual weed business going behind the counter, selling mostly to other employees or American tourists. I'm not sure what type of person asks a gas station employee if they have drugs to sell, but they come to our shop. Once the bosses are gone for the day, we get high in the back. One of the older guys comes up with the genius idea to blow the smoke into the exhaust vacuums, though I'm sure people can still smell it. Then we stumble through work dazed and half-asleep.

We steal iced teas, or Häagen-Dazs if feeling fancy, and eat everything in sight, our faces dusted in sugar and chocolate. Sometimes playing hockey with brooms and crushed pop cans in the back, if the bays aren't full. When even hockey is too boring, we play a game with matches. We pour lock de-icer onto the concrete and throw a match at the puddle from an agreed-upon distance.

The key is to pinch the match between the pack's ends and rip it into the air, all at once, so it stays lit as it tumbles. When the fluid catches, sheets of blue fire swerve across the floor. We laugh and jump back, then pour more, light that, too, go through entire bottles, the little flashes fighting off the cold beyond the big pull-down doors, passing the hours until we can leave.

•

OUR STUDENT CREW DRIVES TWO hours north from Whitehorse into the mountains. I'm not sure exactly where we're going. Matt, the team leader, might know. He's always drumming out complex rhythms on the steering wheel, as if to indicate that he was once a drummer. Or maybe we'll find out once we get to the visitor reception centre. The sky is a cold blue and willows tremble beyond the truck's windows, and Kluane Lake tracks our progress through the last stretch like a serpentine mirror. This student gig with the Department of Environment isn't so bad. We clean up garbage and improve public-access wilderness areas, often camping out in the woods. Now, the five of us, four workers and one team leader, are on loan to the Kluane First Nation to assist at a culture camp celebrating their return to Kluane National Park and Reserve.

The Thechàl Dhâl' Visitor Centre is a wood building off the highway, next to a small parking lot. Matt goes and talks to the lady inside about where the culture camp is. She tells him to keep on down the gravel road that connects to the parking lot. We get back in the truck and I open a bag of corn nuts. Rock music blares on the radio, though I can't identify the band. Potholes and roots jar the truck as we drive deeper into the woods.

Ten minutes later the camp comes into view. Wall tents and firepits. Hanging moose hides. Trucks. Storage tents. A camp kitchen, where smiley old ladies stand on the stoop and wave at us. Off to the side is a field of scrub brush and willow. We park the truck and stretch our legs. I'm stiff from sitting. I break up some trail mix and drink half a juice box. It feels weird coming here for work, like it's not my place. But I'm sure I'll learn as I go.

We haul our gear out to the field and pitch the tents. I've got my own tent, at least, one of Dad's, musty and smelling like his unwashed body and our dogs. Not much privacy, but nylon is better than nothing. We'll be here for seven days.

Matt wakes us up early, my tent wall not doing much in the way of dampening his voice. I've got a spider in my hair, the field overrun with small brown spiders. You'd think this would lessen the number of mosquitoes, but it doesn't. We cook eggs and toast and I try to drink some water. The air's so dry. A constant wind inflates my shirt and tickles my collarbones.

After breakfast, we make brown-bag lunches for the kids. The sandwiches are basic meat and cheese, and could be nicer, but there are many kids and few of us. One juice box per lunch. One apple or orange. One granola bar. We clean up our prep tables after the kids hike into the woods with one of the elders, then we take a long lunch.

Roxanne and I smoke a joint on a mossy hillock in the bush that afternoon. The woods kind of scary. Scabrous branches and dangling lichen and cobwebs somehow undisturbed by the wind. Stoned now, I go back and help out around the camp, setting up a central gathering tent, carrying logs and coolers and whatever else I'm told to carry.

Night comes on slow, twilight lasting hours in the summer. Only the fatigue in my legs lets me know it's getting late. Something about being outside all day. The work's not too bad. Good exercise. Endless access to the outdoors. Card games around the fire. I eat too much bannock slathered with raspberry jam before bed but pretend like I'm only taking my fair share. The sun's a pink blur over the mountain as I zip up the tent and kill all the mosquitoes that came in with me.

By morning everyone is talking about the sheep hunt. One of the boys and some older hunters are in the mountain range to the north, looking for a Dall sheep. Seems like a big deal, this hunt, how they speak of it. The hunt will make him a man. Maybe this is the best way. At least then you'd know.

I clean the cooking area and make bannock for most of the day around a stone-ringed central firepit. One of the ladies from the kitchen brings over plastic salad bowls of creamy batter, one after another. The process gets faster as I learn. Chunk of lard onto the skillet, let it sizzle, spoon the batter into little mounds. One minute to brown, flip them, and so on. There's a paper-towelled plate on a stone next to the fire, and I fill this with pieces of bannock as they finish. Kids from the camp are constantly sneaking over to take some of the still-hot pieces of fried bread, and, as a former sneaky kid myself, I mostly let them.

Whenever I go to the kitchen for ingredients or supplies, I get teased about my whiteness by the old ladies, who seem to know I'm worried about doing the wrong thing. They all laugh and whisper and gesture and then laugh more. I don't get it.

During a lull with the bannock, I watch the stick gambling. Been a while since I've played, must have been way back in elementary school in the Tutchone language classes we'd sometimes get, or maybe one of the culture camps offered to the school. I even get to play a bit. They get me down on my knees next to some younger boys, the blanket over our hands. Each player has a token of some sort — a bead, a stick, a stone — that they keep in their hand. Once the drumming starts, the team with their hands under the blanket begins passing the tokens from one hand to the other. When the drumming stops, the blanket is pulled away and the other team's captain tries to guess which hand each opposing player's token is in. If they guess right, they get a point. Each team seems to have support drummers that drum harder when it's their turn to guess or to hide the token. My team loses pretty quick. I'm rusty. Then it's back to the firepit and the lard and the new bannock batter from the kitchen.

By now I'm getting used to the mosquitoes, the stone-dust wind, the chill in any shadow. If I were to palpate my neck, I might feel the knob there, but I don't.

After the kids leave on the third day, the old ladies give us a moose pelvis and ask us to cut it apart with bone saws. Part of me wonders if they just want to see us do it. The pelvis is huge, but we lift it together and carry it to one of the picnic tables. Smoke rises from the saw teeth as we work. Shards of bone whizz through the air, smelling like burgers. It takes a while, and I don't know what they plan to do with it.

I'm washing dishes in the camp's wooden kitchen after dinner when a bee flies into the spiderweb next to the door. Two of the old ladies notice and come close to watch. We stand there in silence as the bee thrashes and tears much of the web apart but can't get away. A little brown spider crawls from behind the door and latches on to the bee. They struggle a bit longer, swinging back and forth on the silk like a pendulum. Eventually, the bee goes still, its soft fuzz trembling in the wind. One of the ladies says something about the spider eating well tonight, and we continue on with our work.

Around noon on the fifth day, the camp organizer, this pleasant, brown-haired woman with giant hips, approaches me as I'm carrying some water. The sun's high overhead. I'm caked in sweat and dust. She takes me aside off the trail and says that the hunt was a success. Oh, cool. Good for him. Then she says that I and the other guy on my student crew, Lars, have been chosen to hike into the mountains and bring down the meat. The hunters shot the ram after midnight and were too tired to carry it down. The tone of her voice suggests this is an honour. I say sure. I'm wearing board shorts, no underwear, sneakers from Walmart, and I say sure.

Back at the tents, Lars and I get our packs organized. I'm not sure what to bring and don't have much to choose from. I keep the shorts on. The Walmart shoes are the only ones I brought. I put extra granola bars in my pack's side pocket and add another bottle of water. Lars's dad owns an outfitting company, so he's got all the nicest shit: high-shank leather boots, advanced sweat-wicking pants and shirt and jacket, fleece, CamelBak water system. The layers. I am wearing a hoodie. But I've already said yes to going, so I'm committed. After a final look at my gear, I follow Lars out to the parking lot.

We're soon joined by two hunters, who lead us to a crew cab Ford. We drive twenty kilometres north, toward the Canada-U.S. border. At some point, they see a landmark I don't notice and pull the truck into a dried riverbed of circular white stones. The truck hobbles up and down over the riverbed. We drive until it's too steep for the truck, then park. The hunters get their packs out of the truck's box. I stand there nervous. The lead guy has a rifle and sunglasses and dark wavy hair.

From there we go into the trees.

Dense alders hem us in. Branches and trunks criss-cross into one another, and I can hardly see the sky. Slow going. Mosquitoes and black flies swarm much worse than at the camp. Bugs in my mouth, my ears, feasting. The air is all tree sap and loam and dead wood. Tangled poplars and willows sprout up as we get higher. Hiking for hours. Little whiplike branches scratch lines all over my arms and legs as I try to follow the hunters. They don't seem bothered by any of this. At some point the trees thin and then we're beyond them, onto a shale slope of rocks like wafer-thin dinner plates.

It's been steep since the beginning, but now it's *steep*. I wheeze and sweat and struggle to keep up. I haven't mentioned my fear of heights to anyone. Didn't seem appropriate back in the camp, with the nice lady offering me such a special job. Didn't think we would end up this high, figured there would be a trail, though why you'd hunt along a trail, I don't know.

Sharp rocks spill around us as we climb. I keep coughing to clear my throat. When the other guys aren't looking, I climb on all fours, wedging my gloved hands deep into the loose stones for purchase, the vertigo at my temples, feeling like I might fall off the world. On a stone ridge, we take a break. The lead hunter rolls a joint and passes it around. Lars declines, bit of a square, but I go for it. Every time we take a break from then on, the lead hunter rolls a joint and passes it to me.

As we get higher and higher, the hunters begin to talk about the tall creatures that live in the mountains. Humanoid giants the world has forgotten. They don't use the word *sasquatch*, and that they don't makes it seem more real. How these giants snatch a sheep and walk off with it under their arm. I can't tell if they're joking. I'm getting freaked out. I'm remembering Frank, who also did this type of work, talking about a job he'd been on in these mountains, how the guides would not walk farther into a particular valley after dark. Like, they stopped and made camp early and would not go farther for any reason and told him not to either. As day melts to twilight, it seems more and more like they cannot be joking about the giants, that it must be real, that we are trespassers.

The sheep's body is close now, just around the bend. Then around another bend, and another. Please let it be close. We arrive to the butchered animal at the base of a granite cliff — the animal fell off the cliff when they shot it. Purple dusk has settled over the mountains, and I sink onto a boulder to rest and drink water. I shouldn't have smoked all that weed. Stupid. So tired now, woozy and sugar-starved. I eat a granola bar and try to resist drinking more water, as there's not much left. I'm given one of the sheep's skinless red legs and a bag of organs, and I stuff them in my pack as best I can. Lars is also given an organ bag and looks fucking aghast at having to put it inside his mountaineering pack, but he doesn't say anything.

Near midnight, the sky a swollen grey, we begin the hike back. I fall behind, my legs rubber. At one point I bum-slide down a slope, too tired to stand, and a stone the size of a sink rolls by a few inches to my left. I try not to think about it. After a while, pain and fatigue disappear and there's only a vague awareness that I should not stop. And so I go and go and go, just keeping my eyes on the person in front of me, careful not to slip.

We reach the truck around 1:30 a.m. I slump into the back seat, drifting. As we drive, the hunters play 50 Cent over the stereo and rap along but change the word *hell* to the name of their little town up the highway, singing "I'm going through Burwash." They give me a ginger ale and it's the best thing I've had in my life. No one talks beyond the rapping; there's just the music, the drums, the purple horizon.

A fire's been kept burning at the camp, its flames throwing jagged shadows onto the nearby tent walls. Several elders sit around it, drinking tea from an old cast-iron kettle. We join them, widening the circle. The wood burns in a pillar. Pink sky, blue sky. A woman with short curly hair heats oil in an iron pan with cords of rope around the handle. One of the hunters gives her the sheep's heart

and she places it in the pan, gentle, from edge to edge. Bands of
white fat circle the heart like chains, the organ smaller than I expected. "You eat the heart first," she says, and everyone nods, knowing this already. I don't understand, but am too tired to wonder, and
can only listen to the oil sizzle and blink smoke from my eyes and
watch the glow of morning appear over the trees.

•

AFTER CHRISTMAS, THE PET SCAN comes back clear. The radiation treatments were much easier than chemotherapy — light skin
burn, a few minutes each day, no problem. Half my beard isn't re-
growing, but I feel good. The relief. I hope the relief lasts. I'm back
partying with my roommates, tentative at first, not sure I'm allowed
to be stupid anymore. The truth is you are always allowed.

In February, the family goes to Tofino for storm season. Rain
buffets the rental car as Mom drives the cliffside roads to get there.
She's such a careful driver. I always feel 100 percent safe when she's
driving — she never lets anyone else drive her anywhere.

Whenever our family has gone to Tofino over the years and
decades, we've always stopped at Cathedral Grove. This is one of
the last remaining old-growth forests you can easily drive to. How
quiet it is in the shadow of eight-hundred-year-old Douglas firs and
cedars and hemlocks. And each time we go, we stretch from our
cars and walk among the behemoth trees, our heads tilted skyward,
mostly in silence. We take one photo with us all sitting on the
stump of the same tree that fell decades ago, space for everyone,
then get back into our cars.

My aunt has booked this big house on Clayoquot Sound, right
near Chesterman Beach. Must be expensive. We arrive in the rain.
The forest a dark green, droplets on everything, so wet. The house is
made of cedar: cedar siding, cedar roof. Love the smell. The rooms

arc around a deck that faces the water. There's a hot tub and out-door shower on the deck, also cedar, and beyond, a small patch of manicured grass that morphs abruptly into a rough stone shoreline and tidal zone.

We get up early to visit Chesterman Beach. The sand goes for-ever, the shore so long and blue and violent. I take off my shoes to feel it. Wind rips off the ocean and carries waves far up the sloped shore. We keep moving away from the water, then drifting back, then away, then back, as if called. Pastel-blue cloud over the sea. White froth. The trees on the outer edge of the forest curl away from the water as if combed. Everything so cold.

I remember coming here as a kid. Our station wagon full of foam mattresses and coolers and toys and snacks, and Mom with a big perm, stressed out about mountain lions, carrying a stick. Days of driving and camping and then a long ferry ride to the island. Then, finally, here, where the land seemed to end. We'd run into the water and get knocked stumbling by a wave, then flee as the next wave came to chase us up the beach. Transparent disc-shaped jellyfish dotted the sand, and I remember how, when I picked one up, it ran through my fingers like water and fell apart. The feeling as its body poured past my skin.

I stand ankle-deep in the freezing water, the tide moving against my skin.

At night, we younger generation–types pile into the hot tub with beers. Rain falls against the wood roof, the soft patter making me think of a monastery. This side of the peninsula has no wind; the sky is every shade of blue, and water laps calm against the rocks below the house. We drink and splash each other and try to make the tub hotter and hotter, even though we know it cannot get any hotter than it is. Later, we play cards and board games. Then a big family dinner on the long table, everyone elbow to elbow. It's one of those celebrations where no one wants to point out what is being celebrated, but the act of celebrating is important. As much I want to say something at dinner, something life-affirming or grateful, I don't, and I feel weird about the impulse.

Once people head to their rooms for sleep, I walk onto the deck. I've still got my swim trunks on, and I drape my T-shirt over one of the deck chairs. I slip into the hot tub, glad to be alone. My sister and cousin are still up, and they come out and get in, too. We laugh and talk about school. Eventually, they get tired and hot and head off to their rooms. I turn off the light and sit in the dark water, swishing my hands back and forth. I try to turn the heat up again, then rest my beer bottle's cool glass against my bottom teeth. Rain patters onto the roof. The soft noise all I hear. After I think everyone is asleep, even the stragglers, I climb from the tub and go around the side of the house to the deck shower. There's a small lamp high up on the wall, throwing orange light into the rainforest. Hemlock and cedar grow close to the house. Sword ferns crowd the walkway like a low hedge. I run the shower, the water from it hotter than the hot tub, and wash off the chemicals. I've never showered outside, but I've always wanted to. I stand and admire the trees, the owl sounds, the gentle wind. After twenty minutes, I slip off my trunks and keep showering, pretty sure no one will come out on the deck. I shower and shower and don't want to go inside, and the hot water never seems to run out, so I stay there, my eyes on the jungle, and wonder what to do now.

II

STAGE 3A

enlarged spleen;
lymph node involvement;
above and below diaphragm

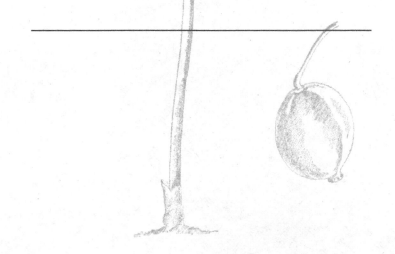

❖

ON THE WALK HOME FROM the bakery, spelt loaf in hand, I look back and see a guy. He's late thirties, salt-and-pepper hair, *very* familiar. He doesn't make eye contact, but if he was a serial killer, would he? A real serial killer would feign disinterest and appear much like a normal stranger, maybe even exactly like one. I run the rest of the way home. Safe in my room with the door locked, I roll a joint and blow the smoke out the window, stinking up the whole place, too worried to go outside. If it wasn't an extreme circumstance, I would never smoke inside. I roll and smoke another joint, and another, and another, then try to sleep. Who was he? I recognized him. From where? Memory so bad of late.

I begin to get concerned.

Smoking on the apartment's stoop the next morning, I get concerned for real. What's the deal with this killer? I'm barefoot on the concrete in front of the door. Cold rain starts to fall, the wind-blown drops landing on my toes.

My lungs ache. All that paper and resin. I keep burning my lips. But this serial killer. I get to thinking about how he'd attack. My roommate, Angie, wouldn't be able to save me. She manages the vagina-waxing place downtown, but she's no martial artist. This killer probably came up in the clandestine services. He'll glide in during the darkest stage of night, having watched me for weeks, knowing me more intimately than I know myself.

I start sleeping with an old utility knife under my pillow. A birthday gift from my dad. There's black weed resin on the blade from scraping my pipes. The first night, I keep the knife folded closed under the pillow. The second night, I keep it open.

If you want to be high all day every day, it's important to plan ahead. Have water, rolling papers, already busted-up flower, at least five lighters, bagged snacks. Small sober patches need to be sprinkled throughout the week for grad school. It's getting difficult. Brain fog. Lethargy. The killer always on my mind.

I've started to forget words. Easy words. Nouns like *balloon* or *pomegranate*. Writing's still going okay, at least. Novel progress. Ideas. But feeling like a fake, basically copying Dave Eggers's *A Heartbreaking Work of Staggering Genius*, and it's so fucking obvious. Anyone who reads the book will know and shame me. Usually writing at 3:00 a.m., or later, the single lamp hot on my eyes, weird auras on the drywall.

I try quitting weed. Again and again, I try. Can't remember the day of the week. And when I run out of weed, I end up kneeling on the carpet looking through the fibres, sure I dropped some earlier. Or I run a playing card or knife along the inside of empty weed bags — the knife works better, yellow crystal dust in a thin line down the blade, carefully scraped into a pipe, so strong, reeling. No one at school has mentioned anything; maybe they do not know. They are so kind to me. And as long as I keep the knife under my pillow and stay vigilant, as long as I consider all the angles.

The killer might be in for a surprise. Can he possibly know I grew up reading every Tom Clancy novel in print? Devouring them. Tradecraft, reversals, secret skills.

I start to place a door trap when I leave the apartment. In case the killer wants to sneak into my room. What you do is fill a small bowl with loose change, and when you leave a room you don't want someone snooping in — the door must open inward — close the door most of the way, kneel down, and put the bowl of coins against the door so anyone who opens it will knock it over. But this isn't everything, no. You leave one coin on the carpet next to the bowl.

•

WE'RE STUDYING THE SHORT FORM with Lorna Crozier. She's brilliant, gentle in the right ways, firm in the right ways. Her husband, Patrick Lane, comes in one day to give a guest lecture. While we do introductions, he says I look like a novelist; it's the best thing anyone's ever said to me. The students in this graduate cohort are all smart and can talk about technique and publish in journals. I try to keep up, writing weird shorts about a drug dealer who made us smoke weed off a homemade contraption of blowtorches, shorts about brewing vodka in university bathtubs, shorts about how the girl I had a crush on in fifth grade told her mom, in front of me, that I was the class clown and how I'd never had someone talk about me in that way.

The paranoia stays. By now I know they are delusions, but I'm still afraid. Each day when I get home, I check the coin bowl and the single coin on the floor, and each day it is unchanged. No one has been in my room, no girls, no friends. Sometimes I forget about the trap and knock the coins everywhere, unable to know for sure if, that one time, the killer *had* been there.

Squads of spiders are the only things sneaking into my room. There must be a gap somewhere in the mesh window screen or baseboard heater. Big spiders, these, maybe the size of a tablespoon. I'll sometimes feel them on me in bed and have to get up, turn on all the lamps, and put socks on my hands to smash them. It's the thing where you have a vague sensation something is on you, a brush, a tickle, and then rationalize that, no, it's nothing, nothing is on you. But recently, when I've turned on the light, there has been a real spider on me. The spiders are real.

I almost never leave the apartment, and when I do go out, like to a bar, I get wasted and sometimes black out. Also doing cocaine with an old Whitehorse friend who is in Victoria for school. He gives it to me for free because he knows my brother, or he feels sorry that I've had cancer, maybe, or he's just a nice guy. And then he and I and whoever else is there yammer and talk in circles for an hour, the drip in my throat like a split-open battery. Then we do more cocaine, and so on, in the way of cocaine, until it's morning and I'm back at the apartment. I take off my clothes and sit at my desk naked, grey light cutting across my legs. I peel an orange, impale it on my thumb and stare at it as the cold juice runs down my arm.

•

I'M AT MY DESK HAVING smoked the last of the weed when I decide to quit. The serial-killer situation tarnished the lustre. Eight years smoking, but I will stop. I say it out loud — "Today, I will stop." — to make it serious and for real. Around four in the afternoon that same day, I'm going through the drawers in my room looking for old bags of weed that might have crystalline residue on the inside. It's fine, it's not a big deal. I hit up my weed guy and buy more, and smoke it all over the next week, miserable, coughing up black slime in the mornings. When this eighth of an ounce runs out, I will stop.

Around four in the afternoon on the next day I decide to stop, I'm going through the drawers again, only now there are fewer old bags with crystalline residue, and the ones I do find have been already scraped clean by my Visa card. I heat my old glass pipe with a lighter until it glows and use an unfolded paper clip to scrape out black resin from the inside. Once I have enough, I put it back into the pipe and smoke it, the glob glowing like a demonic heart at the bottom of a caldera. The high from this recycled goo is a shroud lasting several hours. The taste lingers all day, my tonsils scorched. I'm still high, but it's not the same. Then again, even getting high off real weed is not the same as I want it to be, not the same as it's held in my memory — the hot feel in my lungs, the sense of loss.

After coming down from the black goo, I commit to quitting for real. It's weird how you commit to quitting and then find yourself literally outside on the street having texted your weed guy that you're coming over in a rainstorm. One minute I'm a new man, and the next I'm seven blocks away, speed walking. I get home with the weed and sit at my desk, unsure what happened. Staring at the bag. It smells so good. I know that I'm going to smoke it all. And I do. School and my thesis are an afterthought.

After smoking that new bag, the guilt is so strong I stop leaving the basement suite entirely. My roommate is just living her life, seems to be doing well, though I don't think I'd want to wax vaginas all day, but she perseveres. She's ambitious and organized and will flourish. I need to be organized.

A week later, I am strolling back to the weed guy's apartment. He has such nice weed and always does a little fashion show for the different strains. He's the type of guy who wears only pyjama pants, usually in plaid or various red-striped patterns, and is always eating cereal. When I get there, he'll buzz me up and bring out Tupperware with masking-tape name tags that he's written on in black marker. Blueberry Kush. Lemon Haze. Jack Herer. He lets me smell each strain, palpate the buds, make the hard decisions. And then I'm off with whatever I chose, back to the basement.

Only this time, when I get home, I don't smoke right away. The buds smell so good, but I don't smoke right away. I sit at my desk as spring light plays across half of my computer's screen and do not smoke. I pour the weed into the toilet, stare at it, think about trying to fish it out of the water, but don't, and flush.

With quitting weed, it's important to realize you will not sleep for *a while*. Sleep has been helped along by it for years and that is gone now, so be aware. Also, you won't eat or be hungry. You might get skinny — *it's not all bad*, I think at the time. Boredom will last for months. What was I doing before?

I rationalize that I just need to sweat it out, that weed is fat soluble and lingers in body tissues. I start doing one hour of yoga each morning, even though I don't know how to do yoga. Very limber now. Injured often, especially my neck and back, but very limber. The injuries don't stop me from doing headstands. This is part of the process. During these initial yoga weeks, I keep navigating a perfect maze of logic as to why smoking weed is the solution to how I should quit smoking weed. I sit in the bathtub each night and read or let my head sink below the surface until I can't hear anything except the thrum of the plumbing. Our bathroom's white ceiling has these brown splotches. I wonder if it's nicotine from Angie. I hope she quits. But maybe it's tar from me, the black pipe goo. I sit in these baths and read *Infinite Jest*, because my aunt gave it to me for Christmas. The pages get swollen and fluffy and the cover falls off. Now, there's just my aunt's note on the inner page, saying she hopes I enjoy it — she must not have read this one. I don't think I even asked for the book, but she got it for me and here I am reading it. The story doesn't make much sense. But the parts about the weed addiction, yeah, absolutely.

As sober months trickle by, the memories come. Please leave me alone, memories. I don't want this part. I start meditating and going through each bad memory to, like, feel it and, through this experiencing, let it go, because I've read that somewhere or heard it in one of the guided meditations I listen to. The intensity of these memories, especially junior high, the bullying. Body sensations from back then reappear. Stomach pain. Too hot, too cold. What feels like fever. My immune system really struggling. Seems like I'm always a little sick, especially as July bleeds into August bleeds into September. And I start to wonder about the cancer maybe being back. At first just joking, like *Wouldn't that be something. Wouldn't that be crazy.* What happens is, I get it in my head. Which is always bad.

After a few days freaking out, I go to my doctor with this new revelation that the cancer is back. She says I'm being a hypochondriac and tells me to go home. Maybe she's right. She checks my blood, and it's fine. But blood isn't indicative for my lymphoma unless you're at the stage where your organs start melting, so I ask for more tests. There's resistance. Tests place a burden on the system; they use up vital resources. Blah, blah, blah. Maybe I should just stop being paranoid. Maybe I should just trust her. My family, too, they imply. I persist and persist. I've been somewhat sick for a while now, months. Can't get ahead of it. Can't extricate. All the clarity from not smoking overshadowed by the dread. Finally, the doctor capitulates. Though she doesn't agree with me, if I insist, if I truly insist, she will order an abdominal CT scan. I do insist. A few weeks later, she calls and says I need to come in and see her. I ask why and she won't say. *That's* a feeling.

I go to her office that week and sit on the white paper stretched over the examination table. She soon comes in and apologizes.

The scan showed enlarged lymph nodes throughout my abdomen. There's the sense she's astounded, like how could I have known? And for half a second, I feel vindicated and good. That fades quickly. No sweet victory here.

She treats me differently now. Maybe unsure how I guessed. There is no logic in it, though I look. What matters is the cancer is back, and advanced. Now above and below the diaphragm. I knew, though. *I knew.* But magically knowing is its own problem. Because from then on, you expect to magically know, and when you don't — and you *won't*, almost ever, because you are not magical — you have failed.

•

WHEN CANCER COMES BACK, THEY call the chemotherapy *salvage treatment.* To hear the doctor say it: *salvage.* A term from the naval principle of compensation paid for saving lives and property from a wreck at sea. My salvage is a thing called GDP, which they warn me about from the beginning. Uncharacteristic for them to warn about a treatment — normally they use duplicitous terms like *well tolerated* to describe how hard a chemotherapy might be. But even their warning is not enough. And it's during this first round of GDP that I make a big mistake.

The day of the first infusion arrives, and I go to the cancer centre and sit in the chair for four hours, like always. Dad's come this time, flown from Yukon to assist. The juices flow into my arm, and I brace myself as the heat starts. There's always a fever-like heat with chemo, an under-skin boiling.

They let me leave, and in a haze I take a cab back to the basement suite. Dad wants to help, but there's nothing he can do right now. I need to lie down. I need to be alone. This GDP *is* worse than the other chemo. Worse than my most extreme imaginings.

He goes back to his hotel. Luckily, Angie, my roommate, is at work and won't have to see me right now. I'm bedridden. For the rest of the day, I eat handfuls of benzodiazepines and play a video game, purging demonic evil from abandoned monasteries. Later that night, I lie awake in a pool of sweat and imagine dying. I try not to be afraid, try to envision the feeling of not existing.

Among other medication, they've got me taking antipsychotics for the nausea. Having no experience with these drugs, I take two instead of one. I end up in the kitchen not even sure I'm a person, so dissociated that it takes me five minutes to open the fridge. Then back to bed, on my side, staring at the alley beyond the window. Other houses abut ours, also full of students who come and go and party at all hours; their conversations drift to me, the breathlessness, the trying to say everything at once, like there is no time.

Spring's cold light makes my bedroom look like a charcoal drawing. I hobble from bed to computer chair, then back to bed. Trying to watch movies but losing the thread in the Ativan haze and then five hours have passed. Taking more Ativan, the doctor having given me a truly large amount, enough that I don't need to count them. And then, as the days trickle by, I don't feel any better. Four days, five days, eight days, and realizing I'm supposed to get another infusion on Friday. Already? It can't be. But I think that it is, that it can be. I go over the treatment schedule they gave me, and yes, it seems like there's another infusion coming up on Friday.

Dad looks in my bedroom door on the ninth morning of that first cycle and gets this appalled look on his face. All the muscles warble and take on shapes I've never seen. I'm curled up in the blankets, staring back at him. He's never reacted this way to seeing me. I tell him I left a message with the nurses at the hospital that I'd rather die than get the infusion on Friday, that I'm okay dying and have decided to refuse further treatment and will then die. After that I don't speak anymore.

An hour passes. Dad has been conferring with my sister in the living room, their voices hushed. She came down from Yukon after the treatment to help out. Soon, he peeks into the room again, says, "Hey, maybe we should go to the hospital and see what's up? Just to see how things are going."

The cancer nurse calls back. I don't answer but do listen to her message, her tone scared, saying I should really come to the hospital to chat, to check in. I guess I could. Why not? It doesn't matter, now that I'm going to die. Dad and I sit on the couch to wait for the cab. I'm still mute. I notice a tremor through him, his head moving back and forth, like he's looking for something that is just outside his vision.

"What can I do?" he says, loud. "What can I do? I can't do anything. What can I do?"

So we go to the hospital. I'm still catatonic, my mouth smooth and droopy. There's nothing more to say. All possible reasons to communicate subsumed by one greater reason. The doctor on rotation at the cancer clinic leads me to a bed surrounded by white curtains. This room is right off the main chemo room and it's a deep agony to even be proximal to that space again. Though I can't feel the agony, am just aware of it, like those infomercials where a starving kid is being eaten by a vulture. He smiles often, this doctor, having seen it all. He asks me basic questions that I don't answer. He keeps talking as if I have answered. I'm curled up on my side. They are all very worried, he says. The nurses told him about my voice mail, that I said I was fine dying and would refuse treatment. Why did I leave that voice mail? Why would I say those things in a voice mail? Looking through the folder in his hands, he says my next infusion isn't for two weeks, so he's not sure what I was talking about in that message and I must be making a mistake.

•

IT'S NIGHT AND SHE'S LEAVING and won't be back. I can always tell; there's a chest feel, a static. Yellow light from the parking lot's motion sensor lamp fans through the blinds as she gets her clothes on. My apartment is a small white cube. I sit on the bed as the door closes and can smell her sweat, laundry detergent, sweet lemon from the half-burnt candle on the coffee table. The way she closes the door all gentle. Better she swear and rage. Composure is much worse. Whatever's between us is unnameable, for now. Not even able to get hard the last few times she's been over, no matter what we do, something wrong with me. This is a not the end of anything — it's just leaving.

I sit in the dark and think back to the first date, when she said she had a cold. We were at a coffee shop over on Quadra Street where the tables are shaped like little elephants. She kept coughing and at one point went to the bathroom for a long time, then came back with a look like she was wondering if she should say something. Secrets, I guess. Us with our afflictions — hers worse than mine, mine nothing in comparison. Maybe that's all it was. To be with someone in *greater danger*. I thought it would be perfect. How she'd talk until a coughing fit, then hit her inhaler, flash a cute smile. These are the fantasies of the recently dying. I keep forgetting I'm cured, but all I think of is being with her, with anyone, then dead. I need help. This is not okay.

And in the coming weeks, we'll say cruel things to each other. In the coming months, I'll run into her again and again, this city like a pinball machine where you cannot fully lose your quarter. Her everywhere. And I'll think of the speck of blood she forgot to clean along the edge of my sink that one time after a wild coughing fit in the middle of the night and how I pretended to be asleep, or I'll think of the morning in bed, tangled and resting, blue sky through the open window and warm wind over us with the smell of grass and house paint, when she said, "This is a perfect moment," and we both believed it.

•

I TAKE A SUMMER BREAK from working on the novel and drive five hundred kilometres to a music festival in Dawson City, Yukon. My musician friends have brought a big bag of MDMA with them, and we're all in one friend's house, her father working on the highways. Too many people. A tide of shoes. Mud. Sweaters in balled-up mounds. Everyone snorting or eating little toilet-paper-wrapped parachutes of crystalline brown grit. At first, I only eat some, but later I snort a giant line of it off a ten of hearts, and I am lifted out of my body and telling every person I meet the details of my entire life. There's a black puppy barely able to walk. Cans and bottles carpet the floor. Music rages through the house, and it's impossible to tell time or know what is happening. Land of the midnight sun. Yesterday and today, trapped in a globe.

I'm in the festival tent when I see the woman who, when she was just a child, witnessed me fall into a lake. A family friend. She later confided to my sister that she'd watched me fall in and not told anyone. Not shouted for help, *decided* not to, afraid of what would happen. Such strange, believable logic. I don't know that I remember the drowning, though I can see pale green water, bright sand, my body drifting at the odd angle of someone who cannot swim. And maybe that's a real memory. Part of an old dream. Lake dreams. Swimming dreams. Dad noticed me missing at some point and dove in to save me.

I see this woman outside the main festival tent, and I know she's on a giant pile of psychedelic mushrooms because I saw her upend the bag into her mouth earlier, but I go up to her and tell her

I know about her letting me drown. My intention to be funny, but instead she screams and runs off into a press of bodies and I don't get to apologize.

•

IN HIGH SCHOOL, WE SMOKE from pop cans. We smoke from apples and light bulbs and engineered Gatorade bottles. We smoke from stolen high-school-chemistry graduated cylinders cut with glass drills. One time we are at some guy's house — I don't know this guy — who lives up the hill from Whitehorse and thinks himself a crime facilitator. Small-time weed guy. There's an energy to people who want to be small criminals, an excited movement to the eyes, a way they wear orange or red sweaters. This guy has an old plastic jug he's turned into a gravity bong. I'm with my two buddies, one of whom knows this drug dealer, and we're at his place on a grey-skied Friday night. I drove because I always drive, and I realize at some point I'll need to drive away, but I don't think about it.

We're in the unfinished basement now, where things like this happen. The guy holds a small flamethrower to the weed in the g-bong's glass bowl. Once the flower catches fire, he pulls the top jug up and out of the water bucket, the negative pressure pulling a dense smoke cloud into the chamber. The smoke changes from grey to white to yellow, it's so thick. A colour smoke shouldn't be. And then it's my turn, apparently, because they are all like, "Go, go, go," so I put my lips over the spout to take it all in. Smoke like boiling syrup. My throat cooks. I'm dizzy and bent half over, coughing. I am history. I already want to be away from here. Do I drive? My friend's house where we always crash isn't far. I don't remember.

At some point we leave. Back at the friend's house now, on couches in the basement, the ceiling a blender. I creep into the backyard, where it's cold and dark. Stars dot the sky in incomprehensible strips I don't realize are gaps in the cloud. Rain falls. I lie on the wet grass and close my eyes. Can't keep them closed, though, the spinning even worse if they're closed. So I open them. Black sky in a whirl, all smeared. When I blink, the darkness takes hypermobile forms I can't handle. Thinking, *Is this necessary? Is this what I need?* Oblivion like a black balloon.

All this just to be away. All this unspoken escape.

Unhappy back on earth with school and its cruelties and the guys I stand with in the school's entryway scaring everyone who walks by, and I hate it, but keep them close, close where I can see them.

•

EVERYTHING IS MEASURED: MILLIGRAMS PER kilo of body weight, flow rate, organ burden. Liquids that come in bags within bags, their plastic tagged in black symbols, biohazard, caution, not to be ingested. Nurses so careful with these. They show me the bag and ask, "Is this your name. Is this you?" Yes, yes. It's me from before; it's me from after. The liquids are gold and yellow and cherry red — cell-killing amino acids, antimetabolites originally found in sea sponges, nitrogen mustards, even synthetic derivatives of the wild mandrake. The wild mandrake is called may apple, is called ground lemon. Having white, red, or green flowers. Each part of the wild mandrake is poisonous. Etoposide is extracted from the broad green leaves, then synthesized and brought to people like me in bags within bags. It will damage my DNA and, hopefully, damage it enough.

Chemo at these concentrations requires a Hickman line. There's a perpetual itch where the white plastic tube burrows into the skin above my clavicle, the tube feeding from jugular vein to left ventricle. A scab has built up around the entry point from my constant picking at it. The Hickman is crucial, though, preventing hundreds of needles, allowing transfusions and the type of chemo-therapy that would melt a smaller vein. Released into my heart, the etoposide will do the least damage, but also the most, like every-thing. The wild mandrake in my heart, hunting my blood. Good to begin in the heart with alkylation, with the suspicion I'll be here forever. And as night cools beyond the thick windows that cannot open, I see a claw moon and other buildings' windows, and other moons in them, and other people whose windows cannot open, all looking into a great expanse, unsure what they'll take into their hearts next.

•

I WALK BAREFOOT LOOPS OF the ward at night. It's encour-aged. Moving lowers the risk of embolism or bedsores and speeds up metabolism. My back hurts from being in bed so much. After dinner every day, I unplug the IV pole and drag it with me on my circuits, one hand guiding the pole, the other in my pocket to keep warm. I know this walk by now. Know the pole's single loose wheel and the sound it makes as it passes over the gap near the big double doors. When the IV rig's battery runs low, it emits a shrill beeping, at which point the walk is over. An awful sound, engineered to be noticed. It takes around twenty minutes before the beeping starts, sometimes more, sometimes less. At least I don't have to think about when to stop walking — when the sound comes, I know.

They have me on bags of saline and potassium and various other solutions twenty-four hours a day to keep my kidneys going, and these, too, beep when they are empty.

At least the ward is a circle. Circles are better for walking. They remind me that efforts to move beyond things often bring us back to those same things. In the middle of the circle are the nursing station and drug storage. Along the outside of the circle are the patients' rooms.

I miss home. I miss the quiet of snow.

Other patients pass me as I walk, or I pass them. To walk clockwise or counter-clockwise is a personal choice. There's little traffic, most patients unable or unwilling to walk. I am the fastest walker, the best walker. This shows that I'm fine, that this hasn't destroyed me. As I walk, I look into the rooms with open doors. There are patients propped up by pillows watching tiny televisions that hang from the ceiling. Patients curled into little balls faced away from the door. Patients sitting on the edge of their bed staring off into space, waiting for something to arrive. Many have personal effects along their windows. Plants, blankets, stuffed toys, artwork. I have nothing in my room beyond a computer and some clothes. No part of myself should touch this place. Most of the doors are closed, and I can only guess at who is inside.

In one room there's a young Asian woman, her face swollen into a sphere from the steroids, like mine. We are all so swollen and spherical, our initial variations boiled away to one shiny standard. She's sometimes walking, too. Good. She's strong. It's hard to tell precise age with the bald, but she must be young. Her affliction probably a regular lymphoma. She'll beat it. I feel this. She'll breeze through and not reflect on any of this, and never tell hospital stories to people she meets at parties. But I could be wrong.

There's this thing that happens around other cancer people: they *all* appear strong. They are so formidable. Your own suffering reflected in them. None of these people show any emotion, or they do so only in private. And like this the strength is clear, is manifest. Each time I see other cancer people, I look for something, anything. All the unfathomable miseries of their treatment cycles, the blood, the despair, and their affect flat as a coin, with no outward presentation. So, I call that strong. And when they look at my response, maybe they call that strong, too. Us, all together, *strong*, held up by a hope that we will be last ones here.

•

WHAT HAPPENS IS, WE ALL melt. Afterward, there's quiet. Beads of water glide down windows. Sparrows build nests in MRI machines. The dams go, little cracks growing into big cracks. The world soon scoured, lakes and oceans pooling in the lowlands like great blue mirrors. Food blackens and begins to crawl and wonder. It's nice to think that someone, somewhere, survives via miraculous remission, but no one does. No chance. All percentages approach zero. Everyone is gone. This is how it must happen. Great forests spring up around buildings and military bases. All the blank televisions reflect light at these new plants and fuel further regrowth. Endless parking lots of bones bleach in the sun. Then nuclear disasters. Sure. When the fail-safes themselves fail. Darkening plumes of heavy elements coating regions like gauze. Inevitable. If we hadn't *all* had it, who knows, could have been averted, but we all did have it. The animals grow extra horns and teeth and limbs if they must, and in time they adapt, avoid the burning areas, live only in zones of achy yellow sun and soft fields of warping grass and forests where water is the only noise, like we always hoped to.

•

AFTER THE STEM CELL TRANSPLANT and grad school, I am broke, unemployed, and look like the kid from the movie *Powder*. But I'm alive, back in remission. For a term, I teach a workshop at the university, but the tenured professors come back from sabbatical by spring, and that evaporates. In the meantime, I max out my credit line and liquidate a mutual fund I'd been putting fifty bucks a month into for four years. The fund not mature, taking the loss. For months I send out resumés and don't hear back. I start with good jobs that pay well and work my way down to a hair above fast-food joints.

After several dozen applications with no interview, I remove the M.F.A. from my resumé — then even the B.A. — and immediately get called back by a grocery store's deli. There's a rainstorm the day I bus there to speak with the manager, water flowing in rivers down the street, the sky a grey wound. He meets me in the cereal aisle, centring boxes as we talk, and, without directly looking at me, asks what I'm expecting for pay. We're surrounded by Corn Flakes and Lucky Charms. I ask for more than minimum wage, and he offers fifty cents more. Okay. It's not enough to live on — nothing is — but I'll need less from my parents. The stress of asking them for money again and again fills my mouth with ulcers, and I keep doing it.

Now, to sell chicken wings, stuffed olives, pepperoni, Greek pastries. And meat. Mountains of it. We have sliced meat in the display, but customers want it fresh. Black Forest ham, honey ham, prosciutto, soppressata, capicola, fat-rimmed pancetta, speck, bleeding roast beef, every kind. So much meat. It coats me. Is a mist. And they always want it thinner. Thinner, they say. No, thinner than that. I cut a piece and bring it to the counter, hold it up. They look, head tilted to one side, indicate no. No, that won't do. Charcuterie, guests, entertaining. I understand, right? It must be thinner. See-through, paper thin, falling apart. And then it will be too thin, turning to pink slurry against the slicer blade, and they'll say well, no, not that thin. Faced with the limitations of tissue.

Panic attacks start around this time. Tunnel vision. Standing in the food freezer until they pass. I don't take a sick day for three years. There aren't sick days.

Working with high-schoolers again. Blast from the past. Some middle-class or rich kids, their parents making them work to build character. But also other kids, the no-choice kids. Helping families with rent. Paying their own. Saving for who knows what. One girl is sixteen. Adopted from Russia, then into the system, group homes, bounced around. Fired from the last six jobs, can't understand why. Says she'll stop showing up, smoke weed, steal. Failing all her classes at school. She asks me if she should drop out. No. Try and finish. But it's so hard, the school, the math, the assignments. Why is it so hard, she wonders. What is different about her? Why can't she succeed? And I stand there, having had every advantage, ham all over me, and don't know what to say. I want to say you need this job. I want to say don't drop out of school, find good people, get a certificate, something, anything, because when you age out of the system these institutions won't give a fuck about you, if they even do now, and you will land wherever you fall. Instead I ask her to get the chickens from the oven, the bell is going, make sure the seasoning doesn't rub off on the rim of the bag.

And soon she quits, or gets fired. Don't see her for months, until one day I'm taking the bus, and she's there and waves and says we should hang out some time, and I lie and say, "Sure, let's do that."

•

ON DAY TEN OF MY stay at Vancouver General Hospital, I wake with hair all over my pillow. There's an itchiness to the pillow hair that wakes me and has been waking me for days. When a nurse checks on me after breakfast, I request that they cut my hair off. She nods, maybe expecting it, noticing the hair everywhere. She's seen this day before, hundreds of times.

After lunch a different nurse comes to my room with a hair clipper in a brown plastic case. Better to do it and be done, I figure, though I've been postponing. What is hair? What is its power? As she plugs the trimmer in, I use the bed's controls to raise the back up, making a face for her like it's very funny for me to use the controls, since I'm so strong and don't actually need them. Using the controls a lot now. The first few days weren't so bad, before the stem cell chemo took effect. At one point even using the ward's dusty recumbent bicycle which, judging from the looks I got, no patient in history had ever used. Dragging the IV pole to the bicycle now seems impossible.

The room's cold, or I'm cold. I scoot to the edge of the bed with my arms crossed tight over my chest. I haven't buttoned my shirt in days, even though I'm always shivering, almost as if being fully clothed in this place would be capitulation, like saying *I am a member of society*, which I most definitely am not anymore. My skin is white as paper and covered in bruises.

The nurse — so cute, button nose — places a bucket at my feet and asks me to lean forward. She starts at my neck, her other hand holding my forehead. Back and forth go the clippers, and brown tufts of hair swirl past my eyes in helixes. Her hand is on my shoulder, then my head again, steering the clippers. How she brushes against my ear. Up here, I'm touched all the time but never like this, never like how you might be touched in the real world. She takes off the guard near the end, to get closer, and I try not to sigh. Rain light bathes the room, diffuse and cool. Beyond the window it's overcast, thick clouds in the air like wings. I say she should be careful with the unguarded trimmer, that my blood won't clot. We laugh about exsanguination. The bruises on my legs are the biggest, some the size of apples. I'm anemic. And now truly bald. And hoping she won't leave yet, that she's a perfectionist and will keep trimming, that we can be here and pretend for just a little longer.

•

AT NIGHT I SIT IN the wheelchair next to my bed and stare out over the glowing city. I have zero white blood cells, but I'm eating again. I may also have *C. diff,* and so I don't infect my roommate, with whom I share a bathroom, there is a small steel dish mounted beneath a hole in my wheelchair. I must call the nurse, and she comes in gowned and masked and gloved and collects the dish, takes a sample, rinses the dish, and puts it back into the wheelchair. I am mustard gas and platinum now, alchemical, inhuman. I curl into the blankets and pull them over my face and try not to move or think, the negative air vents whooshing overhead, cold IV tubes wrapped around me like kelp. I don't know what the lesson is.

•

AFTER THE STEM CELL TRANSPLANT, I fly to Yukon to visit my parents. The plane lands around sunset, and the pink sky reminds me of being young and whole. Mom picks me up, and we hug and talk about the dogs and how everyone's doing. So good to be home, so good to have the truck pull into the driveway and see the stacks of lumber and bones and tools and old cars, just like I remember.

The next morning everyone is at work, and I sit outside on the deck. Warm sun washes through the pines. Grass sways in the wind, unkempt, wild. I can taste the sunscreen's coconut and silver. I'm hairless and shouldn't be outside, but don't care. The sun filters red-gold through my closed eyes; the deck sizzles under my feet. Two huge stands of willow shadow the garden, their leaves spinning. Birds speckle the air: White-winged Crossbills, Tree Sparrows, chickadees, all jostling on hanging seed houses. Whistles. Orchestrations. Ravens glide high overhead, coming down only to steal moose bones that haven't yet been taken by something else. The dogs chase after them. Shep is the most protective, a Bernese cross, his hair never shedding properly and always stuck between seasons, old soul, my favourite. Higher still, eagles, Peregrine Falcons, clouds like sheer white scarves.

Over past the greenhouse, we used to cut dead wood with our little hatchets, and a tree once fell on my brother's shoulder. Next to the shed, we fired guns into planks of wood drawn with spiral targets. And there the old station wagon got parked, its engine dead, we siblings in it after school, before Mom and Dad got home, curls of weed smoke in the air, the seats so familiar, the feeling of each road-trip vacation still in the upholstery and wood panelling and whorls of dust.

Beyond the willows there's a fenced field of potatoes, carrots, wild raspberries, and rhubarb. That old fence. Mostly collapsed now, one side the shape of a sine wave. Then there's a small greenhouse of tomatoes and cucumbers. Then the bat houses. Then a solitary saskatoon berry we planted over the grave of our dog, Laika, named after the first dog fired into space.

Near the driveway sit the ancient sheds where my father hangs meat and skins wolves in the winter. Sheds bristling with augers and flamethrowers and machetes and traps and saws and toolboxes and fishing rods and old boat motors and animal pelvises and every other thing in the world. They are his, and he knows each piece of them.

The three-walled woodshed is older than me and half-filled with logs stacked on a bed of hay where the dogs sleep. There's not enough wood for winter, not yet. Dad will go next door with his chainsaw and help the neighbour clear land for her horses. He never cuts on our land and will find someone who needs an area cleared. Will work for the wood. Will come to an agreement so our forest sits and grows, and small trees cast bigger and bigger shadows and everything gets older but remains the same — as if that were possible.

•

SHE'S PERCHED NAKED ON THE flower-print chair I got at
Salvation Army for sixteen dollars. The curtains are open just
enough for her to blow smoke out into the night. Probably too
young for me, but here we are. When she asks if I want to smoke
weed, I nod. I lean out the window gap when it's my turn to exhale, her ribs against me, cold air on my ears. Heat radiates off her
skin. I'm surprised she likes me. She always laughs at my jokes and
falls asleep in one second. Otherwise, she seems to get drunk five
days a week and smoke weed all day. I never go out drinking with
her, other than that first date. Mostly, she just comes over. This
being some of the first human contact I've had since second cancer,
though not a relationship.

She tells me that she was a dancer and hurt her back, and I say
she should try to dance again, in whatever way doesn't hurt, if it
makes her happy. Seems like she just got out of a five-year relationship. Makes sense. How she touches me the way you learn to touch
the one person you are with forever. I work to be okay with it, the
feeling of us being pretend. This can't last or hold still, but I don't
want her to go. After the first night she stays over, I'm sitting on
the edge of the bed in the ash-colour dawn, scanning the room for
my underwear, when she asks, "How are you single?" I blank for a
moment at this. What? Then I say some obvious lie like "I've been
busy." Then I think about it all day. She tells me to put art on my
walls, get plants, anything, my place looking like a mental hospital,
though she doesn't use that phrase. I will get things eventually, I
will have continuity, but not while we are doing this. I can't ever
sleep when she's in my bed, though it's nice. Instead, I stare at the
ceiling and get tickled by her hair against my shoulder, her body all
curled up, the gentle breaths making me feel like a person.

•

FOR THE FIRST FEW MONTHS at the deli, I'm a closer. I work until just after nine. The job is strange after being in academia, because you need to actually work all the time. They want eight hours of work each day, if you can believe it. Breaks are timed outside of that and unpaid, so I'm there for over nine hours, five days a week.

The deli is part of a grocery store in Cadboro Bay, the bus trip there taking twenty minutes, sometimes thirty, or the bus is late and I stand at the stop with my mouth all dry from the stress. Cadboro Bay is one of Victoria's nicest neighbourhoods, but the bus goes through Victoria's *actual* nicest neighbourhood: Uplands. It's a neighbourhood of estates. Some are visible from the street; some are hidden behind tall hedges, their dimensions unclear. A lot of glass and flowers and Land Rovers. Far as I can tell, there's only one bus stop in the whole neighbourhood. Because why would they need more? Each day I bus through Uplands to my twelve-dollar-an-hour job.

The people I work with are good, at least. There's Emily, who's been here a while. Amanda, also here a while, actually close to my age. Then the new people, like me and Sydney and Matthew. Lots of turnover. Jobs aren't fun, so people leave them. The deli manager will always interview a girl if she's pretty and he says as much. I'm overqualified, but I need the money. Others are overqualified. There is no such thing as being overqualified.

I haven't really worked a job like this before, the day-in-day-out brutal kind. After my undergrad, there was the year off, getting too drunk up north in the snow. I worked then, too, but mostly jobs where I'd hammer nails or hike in the woods. Then came grad school. Then cancer again right after that, defending my thesis between bouts of chemo, being all fucked up. The bone marrow transplant that summer. And it's weird, because part of me expects the deli job to, at some point, *end*, but it doesn't. You expect something to happen with jobs like this, as stupid as it sounds. You expect someone to step in and stop the pointless toil. But of course no one does. Or that's just me being spoiled — yes, probably. People do this their whole lives, is something I'm realizing. They have a bad job that pays them poverty wages, and they just do it forever until they die. And now that's me.

I start getting symptoms.

At first, I think the symptoms — stomach pain, mouth ulcers, tunnel vision where the borders of the room ripple and turn into mist — are some new kind of cancer. I mean, why not? Could be. Could very well be. The mouth ulcers especially. I cannot eat solids for days, the pain so intense. My doctor, looking at these giant ulcers, calls them "tonsillar debris," which I don't think is a real phrase. She refers me to an ear, nose, and throat specialist. The wait is four days. I assume she now says any test I need is cancer related, because I seem to leap every line and never wait for anything. I'm fine with it. I do not feel an ounce of guilt.

So I go see this specialist, and he does his examination and says that nothing is wrong with me. Okay, sir. What about all these terrible symptoms? What about the agony?

But the deli job continues. We work at high volume all day. If you've never worked in a commercial kitchen, it's difficult to understand. All day, in these kitchens, you are either making things dirty or cleaning. That's it. The meat slicer *whirs*. Dishes pile up. Steel bowls with the remnants of egg salad and tuna salad and ham salad get stacked like rubble. The ovens are going constantly. Customers swarm the counter.

Weekends, we workers go to the bar or to someone's house to drink. We become friends. The other employees are kind and funny, most of them with undergraduate degrees, also struggling. A lot of high-schoolers work at the store, but I don't befriend or hang with them because it's too weird. The management is all old people with high school diplomas, because back then you just went to high school for this line of work. The people opening the deli need to be there at 5:00 a.m., and they *still* come out drinking. Especially Emily, very courageous, young still. I'm just old as shit. Twenty-seven feels fucking old to slice ham. The shame makes it hard.

I get so tired. Days blur. Months pass. Years. I don't even consider getting a better job. Get drunk when you can. Search for sex. This is all there is. Being mesmerized. Not once do I think *I can do better*. I clock in and clock out and persist.

After a disastrous fallout with one girl, I start dating again. I'm kind of in love with various girls in the grocery store itself, but don't pursue them. Better to keep things separate. I'm trying to be prudent, using the apps. Some women *are* willing to have sex with twenty-seven-year-old deli employees — it's a confusing time. On the one hand, I'm coming to terms with being wounded enough to be attractive or something, or at least tall. I'm trying to bring my self-esteem up. I've got this idea that if I don't make lots of money, I have no value. All I do is slice meat at the deli, work out at the gym, chase girls, and go drinking. I'm lonely. But there's always an interpretation, a framing. There's artistic mystique. There's mentioning I taught at the university. This isn't permanent; it's a hiccup. This will be good material.

Scheduling for the job constantly changes. I start with Monday–Tuesday as my weekend. After several months, I get Tuesday–Wednesday. After a year, I get Wednesday–Thursday, after another year, Thursday–Friday. Getting the actual weekend off is beyond imagining. I can't demand it or earn it. The managers just say no. What are weekends? I don't know. I don't sync up with any of my gainfully employed friends. I am out of rhythm, living in a poverty shadow world.

Finally, they put me in the basement to make sandwiches. Good. No management in the basement, and the cameras are pretend. Down there I use my phone in defiance of the unhinged pogrom the owner's son has going on upstairs against phones. I have a sandwich quota, but beyond making my fifty or sixty or seventy sandwiches each shift, they leave me alone for most of the day. Another benefit of basement duty is I don't have to close. Closing sucks. If anything is fucked up when the managers arrive at five in the morning, it's the closer's fault.

Each morning they give me a list of what they want sandwich-wise. Say, ten ham, fifteen turkey, twelve roast beef, and so on. I make the sandwiches with my phone propped up against the foil wrapping machine, watching YouTube videos about obscure video games or listening to music. The list also has wraps on it, which is too bad. Wraps are way harder to make, so I only sometimes do them. I make myself sandwiches whenever I feel like it. Roast beef for the most part. We roast our own beef in the oven, rare, then slice it paper thin. It's so far out of my price range, it's funny to eat it all the time. Whenever a customer orders roast beef, sees the price tag, and stashes it in an aisle after deciding they can't afford it, I claim the bundle when one of the grocery employees brings it to us to sort out. We can't resell food that's been in the clutches of a customer, so we often take it for ourselves.

At least we get free food, especially if working mornings when all the expired cheese comes back. Imported cheddar from England. Goat cheeses made in caves by monks. This grocery store caters to expensive tastes, but those one-day-expired cheeses still get pulled. Eating pretty good, all things considered. Breakfasting on twenty-dollar omelettes. The Gouda. The Camembert. I'll take any expired nut butters, too. Bread. Cereal. I sometimes give stuff to the homeless guy with horrific toenails who rides my bus at night. I should give him more, or try to plan some strategy with him, but he's only on the bus sometimes, and it's hard to predict, and he kind of freaks me out. The store trashes an absurd amount of food. I've heard about this in the news, the idea that we *can*, in fact, feed everyone, but to see it is grotesque. We really fucking can feed everyone. Even then, what we take home has to be kept secret, the owner always prowling for thieves who deprive the Dumpsters of his goods. I simply cannot throw out such expensive food. So I hoard cheese in my fridge, shaving off mouldy sections as they appear, totally dedicated to the luxury.

At night, when I take the bus back through Uplands, I can see into all the mansions. The darkness makes it easy, and they have so many windows. People in vaulted dining rooms at long wooden tables. Candlelight. Knit sweaters. Chandeliers. Drinking wine in cups the size of melons. Three or four Land Rovers are always parked out front. I sometimes imagine walking into one of these parties. I'd hop off the bus, even though there are no stops, and walk inside the house still in my stained deli shirt. The people at first shocked — who is this guy with a red-pepper logo on his shirt? But I say something charming and unexpected, and everyone laughs. I'm in. We all get along. I'm given cheesecake. I'm given truffle oil. I'm offered a seat and part of a baguette, and if I keep talking and it's a story they've never heard before, a story they have never even imagined, no one will bring up that I don't belong. This goes on all night until the candles burn low and people's eyes soften and everyone falls asleep where they're sitting.

•

THREE MONTHS AFTER THE STEM cell transplant, Dad has a heart attack. He was out at the lake working on the cottage when the chest pain started, the fatigue. But he kept working, of course. The dog freaking out, aware somehow. Dad had a nap to see if it might all blow over. Still not feeling well. One of his buddies helping him out there drove him the hour back to Whitehorse. The hospital tried to send him home like it was nothing, but Mom wouldn't have that. She got them to do an ECG, her nurse instincts suspecting. Always was a good nurse. And they had him on a plane to Vancouver that evening, as there are no heart surgeons in Yukon.

I take the ferry from Victoria to Vancouver that weekend. Back in Vancouver, our city of medical crises. The other siblings are already at a hotel on Robson that gives discounts for family members of medivacs from Yukon. It's two days after his bypass surgery and we four kids take a cab to see him — Angela and Alex, the younger twins, are done their degrees now and back in Yukon, working for the government; Jessica, our older sister, is a nurse at the hospital in Whitehorse.

At least Dad is in St. Paul's and not Vancouver General. Not sure I can go back to VGH so soon. Then again, St. Paul's seems old and dusty as the cab pulls up, all brick and decay, maybe not the best place. The hallways seem to swell and contract around us as we walk in and find an elevator. Vancouver General would have been better.

We track him down in a shared room on one of the upper floors. He's got the blankets thrown back, bandages all over his chest. I go in with just Angela, so as not to have too many people in the room at once. He's half-asleep, looking ragged. Being back in a medical setting is giving me nausea. Bleach. Shiny floors. He wakes up and says our names, disoriented. Must be on lots of drugs. Bisecting the chest plate can't be easy and the aftermath must hurt like hell. We say hi and try to do little partial hugs and arm squeezes that don't touch his chest. Bruises cover his entire right arm and shoulder. Strange. That wasn't where his surgery took place. The whole arm a network of purple and black lines where the veins have burst. What is going on? Jesus Christ.

My sister says something in a casual tone, trying not to be dramatic. "You look kind of bruised, Dad." He says it hurts but isn't clear on what's happening or what has happened. Is the arm thing something to do with the surgery? I can't tell. I know only cancer. He begins to mumble that his IV was hurting a lot and going into his arm. Oh. I get it. An interstitial IV, dislodged from the vein, fluid going into tissue that has no space for it. But for how long? Must've been hours. Is no one checking up on him? The pain from that, saline in the skin layers. That's bad. I ask about his pain level. It seems high, because he's normally Mister Never-Expresses-Pain, but now he grimaces. He's not wearing his partial either, so all the missing teeth from hockey add to the impression of pain.

A nurse comes in and we ask about the IV. She deflects and says they've sorted it out. What a mess. When that happens with chemo drugs, you get chemical burns, necrosis — I've never seen it happen for longer than a moment without being addressed.

We make other small talk and try not to stare at the bruises. Talking about the room, about his food. All through my stay at the hospital in the summer, he encouraged me to eat the food, saying it couldn't be as bad as I said. But here, in this shabby room, he grabs my hand and says, "You were right about the food." And that's all he has to say. I'm sure it's just as bad here, sure this whole system is backwards and upside down.

Later that night, at the hotel, Jess says she got us tickets to see The Weeknd at the Orpheum on his *Kiss Land* tour. She got us four in the nosebleeds, but it's still cool. I like cocaine sex music as much as the next guy. We don't drink or anything beforehand, as there's not much time between buying the tickets and having to go to the venue. We're rattled, I guess. By the things that keep happening to us. From the beginning, our family's been lucky with illness, and I was the only one beset. But it couldn't last forever.

The theatre smells like weed. Ushers bustle about looking for the people causing the smell. We find our seats, and they are far back, up against the wall, but the venue isn't massive. BANKS opens the show. I've never heard of her, but she's good, can handle big high notes live without major backing tracks and dubs. The guys in front of us are on a lot of cocaine and acting stupid, sitting, standing, sitting, standing, asking where The Weeknd is, they don't care about this bitch, when is he coming on?

But eventually he does come on, and it's good. We're all standing to see better, me so recently almost dying, our father currently doing the same, but we four still bobbing our heads to the heavy bass, trying to have fun.

●

I'M IN THE MEAT DEPARTMENT cooler looking for a bin of chickens when one of the butchers comes in with both hands in his apron's stomach-height pockets. White plastic bins of various meats are stacked on shelves around us. Buckets of sauce. Marinades. Steaks. Fish. But hanging pigs take up most of the space. They have hooks through their feet and swing gently in the fan-cooled air. I keep bumping into the pigs as I search for the bin I need.

"You know what I like to do when I'm stressed?" says the butcher from behind me, in a tone that makes it clear he isn't looking at me. "I like to come in here and punch the pigs. Feels good on your knuckles." He throws a right cross at the nearest pig, then a left hook, an uppercut.

I think he's joking. I nod and agree that it must feel good, that their skin is very similar to our own.

I walk back to the deli with the chicken bin, thinking. A guy in the grocery department has died. At first all I heard was that someone who works at the store died. Then I realized it was the guy

trimming vegetables near the bay doors late at night as I'm closing
up. Quiet guy. Always smiled, but never said anything. They found
him on the rocks near the shore around Willows Beach, fallen off
some embankment or cliff. Head injury. Tide came in and drowned
him, or he was already dead, unclear. Some of the guys in grocery
conjecture suicide, that he was wasted, or they knew he was drunk
that night, or something. They say he was an alcoholic, depressed,
all this stuff, but I have never spoken to him or really seen him
talk to anyone at work and am wondering how they know so much
about his life.

There's a new guy in the deli, just out of high school, who is
always stoned. This kid is also an alcoholic, or so he tells me. Bleak
to hear it from someone so young. Usually, teenagers have years of
denial before anything like the word *alcoholic* leaves their mouth.
But he's young, and young people drink, and say unexpected shit
they're too young to say. One day, he comes into work so drunk he's
not even aware what's happening until a few hours later. He leans
against the wall in a daze or hides in the bathroom most of the
morning. We all know he drove to work. Not good. I try to squeeze
in guidance when I can. He goes on about how he's a fuck-up and a
mess and can't really extricate himself from these issues. I'd rather
he deflect and act like it's no big deal. How can he already know all
this about himself?

A willowy girl has been coming to the store a few times each
week and always buys stuff from the deli. Very thin, she's draped
in colourful blouses and trousers. She's a bit weird when we talk at
the deli counter, but not in a bad way. There's something about the
words she chooses. She has giant eyes and long red hair. Tall girls
aren't usually my thing, but I rush to get there first when she lines
up. I haven't had anything successful in a few months, girl-wise,
and it's nice to flirt again. We have this exchange where I'm talking
about how a cheese we sell has a stupid name and how companies

must think of random words to name their cheeses, and then she says the cheese is actually named after a mountain, and she knows this because she's ridden up the mountain on a horse while travelling through England. A few weeks later, she's again at the counter for cold cuts. I get her the sliced turkey and ring it up. As I give her the bundled meat, our eyes catch, and I get a lump in my throat. How long since a real lump? I can't remember. Sometimes there is a clear moment to ask for a girl's number, so I ask for her number and she says sure. I give her a yellow sticky note and one of our deli pens, and she scribbles the number down. It feels good to be nervous in a constructive way.

That Friday we meet at a coffee shop off Hillside for a few hours. She tells me she models for local magazines and has two giant pet rabbits. So expressive, her voice echoing around the coffee shop. But it's not right. I want it to be right, though, want to squeeze whatever's there into the appropriate feeling. I go on another date with her a week after that, because one date is unfair. And the second date also isn't right, and I let her know. She keeps on coming into the store, but we don't talk anymore.

I try to not hit on customers going forward.

Employees get hired and leave. People squabble about being made manager or assistant manager or shift supervisor. I avoid all this and try to eat as much free food as I can while at work to save on buying groceries.

Whenever we deli workers eat food while in the deli — extra meat from the slicer, cookies fresh out of the oven, day-old sandwiches — we duck down behind the cutting board so customers and security cameras can't see us. The work is fast and physical, and we get hungry. We're not allowed to eat in the deli, of course, so they say, but I'll be squatting there with a mouthful of ham, and Sid will drop next to me eating a cookie. There's a gravity to the area behind the cutting board. Emily might join with some of the gross

European bologna she likes. Matthew tends to arrive with spicy salami. And we're all squatting in the shadows where things are a bit quieter, eating, talking. I have this idea for a television show about a deli, and the place behind the counter where people crouch to eat is like its own dimension. This becomes a major pattern through the seasons. People feel safe behind the counter, right? So each episode there'd be characters down there doing monologues or taking journeys into the psyche. How it would work is, the lighting would change to a gauzy, dreamlike yellow when people squatted behind the counter, to alert the audience. Sounds of customers and air conditioning would muffle. The camera would move in close. And it's *there*, in that safe place, that the most important parts of the show would happen. Like the character development. Like where you learn about the new guy's past in the military or the old timer's broken-up marriage or someone being abused, and people watching the show would wonder when the next segment with the characters crouched down eating would be. Even the characters would understand the significance, sometimes having to stand up because they aren't ready to say the important thing that squatting behind the cutting board with a piece of ham in their hand would entail. And then you'd wonder what it was, their truth, and keep wondering until it all came back around and the lights yellowed again and everything went almost quiet.

•

MATTHEW IS EYEING THE PILE of meat scraps. At the end of every closing shift, there's a pile on the cutting board, a blend of everything we sell — ham, salami, beef, chicken — now united by our attempt to gather all the refuse so it can be pushed into the garbage. Slowly at first, then faster, Matthew begins stuffing the pile into a transparent work glove. As the glove fills, it begins to look like a see-through, living organism. He ties off the end and begins to prance it around the cutting board, saying, "This is Meat Glove. Nice to *meat* you." Vocalizing Meat Glove's plans for the future in a little meaty voice. It's a big hit. We all fall for Meat Glove.

Soon, other staff start making Meat Glove at the end of the day. Even I make Meat Glove sometimes.

When I don't make Meat Glove, I like to build small ham-centric dioramas or sculptures. Meat Glove isn't the *only thing*, okay? I'll cut heart shapes out of scraps of Black Forest ham and arrange them into a bouquet with toothpick arrows stabbed through them. Or craft a gingerbread man from ham. You can do a lot with meat. Different meats give you textures and colours to work with, a full palette.

Meat also gathers and combines in the slicer, though not into anything orderly like Meat Glove. No, the slicer turns it into a pink slurry that finds its way into all the nooks and crannies and moving parts of our most important tool. Some meats make more slurry than others. The dry schinkenspeck-type salami don't liquify easily. But the soft processed hams — the Black Forest, the honey, the real pressed ones you aren't sure how they stay together — they become a gel when squished or sliced thinly enough. A pink-white gel that mixes with the red myoglobin from the roast beef and the even squishier, juicier gel of the bologna people always want sliced thinner than is possible, and all these get combined in the recesses of the slicer. You need to get your fingers way up inside to have a hope of cleaning it properly at the end of the day.

Cleaning has its risk, but we follow the rules. We all cut ourselves on the slicer at some point. With new employees, I wonder if they will be the type of people who cut themselves early in their deli career or late. Most of the high-schoolers are the early type, brash, wanting to not seem stupid; they come upstairs from using the even more dangerous slicer in the basement, their hand swaddled in paper towel, and we all just nod, understanding. I was a late guy.

The upstairs slicer is newer and has a blade guard, so even with the cover plate off, it's hard to sever anything. The downstairs slicer has no guard. When you take off *its* cover plate, about eight inches of blade sits there exposed. You need to understand that it's a giant circular scythe and hold that perspective. Don't slip. Don't fall.

The managers often talk about other delis, delis out in the wild, and what they're up to. There's this idea that we are in competition with the other delis. I guess we are. The managers will reconnoitre other delis, spy on the types of meat they sell, the promotions they do. It's dumb. They discuss delis that aren't even in our town. How they know about *these* delis, I have no idea. Maybe there's a deli forum online somewhere with all the scuttlebutt, a special place where lowly service staff convene. One manager swears he's heard about a guy falling into a slicer blade with his wrist and bleeding to death right there in the deli. Says it was a remote location, no ambulance, a deli in the woods or something. We're supposed to always wear a chain mail glove when using the slicer, but no one does. There's no time. You switch between jobs too fast and can't input food codes and prices into the scales with the chain mail on. And for cleaning, when we *do* have the time to wear it, we still don't wear it.

I don't cut myself for the first year. A real good run. When it finally happens, I'm closing alone, it's Saturday, and I've got the whole deli clean and bleached. As I'm spraying some of the pink mystery sanitizer onto the slicer blade, my right index finger slips. I don't register the slip right away. Then comes the sting of sanitizer pouring into the wound. It went through so clean. Right along the finger's pad. Blood wells up and patters onto the beautiful clean slicer. I scramble for paper towel. Then a bandage, a second bandage. Our mystery pink sanitizer appears to be an anticoagulant. I strap a blue nitrile glove over top of the Band-Aids and try to finish the cleaning checklist. Five minutes to close. No time. I get all the blood off the slicer and the counter, throw away the Band-Aid wrappers. The blue glove has filled up with blood like a water balloon. I layer a second glove over the first to prevent any spillage I'm trying to mop one-handed, but the exertion of cleaning has my heart pumping and the cut bleeds and bleeds. One of the guys from grocery sees my plight and helps finish the mopping. What a saint.

And then I'm running to the break room for my backpack. There's only one bus every half hour this time of night. No cold vigil in the darkness for me. Can't do it. I hit the salted air outside and catch my breath. A chill is sweeping in off the ocean. I keep the gloved hand elevated as I run, and from the corner of my eye I see the big wash of bus headlights break around the hedgerow of the nearest corner. But I get to the stop in time. I'm wheezing. I tumble into one of the rainbow velvet seats as the driver dims the lights and accelerates. Up the hill, then past the lion statues at the entrance to Uplands. I'll be home soon, to deal with the cut. The hand is curled in my lap, stinging. I won't want to unwrap it once I'm home. I know this. I'll stand in the shadows outside my bathroom listening to the neighbour's television and not wanting to look at the cut, but after a minute will peel off the glove with that uncertain gentleness we use for injuries too long out of sight, when we both know and don't know what's there.

•

DURING THE BONE MARROW TRANSPLANT, I have a roommate. Some of the patients on the ward don't have roommates, but I think that's only for when having one would kill them. This roommate of mine is older, forties, maybe fifty. Dark hair. Fit. A well-to-do gentleman. A big partition curtain separates our two corners of the room. We each have a bed, our IV rig, a bedside dresser, and a tiny TV set hanging off the ceiling that only has, like, The Food Network and CBS.

Throughout the day, my roommate and I rustle past the curtain to use the bathroom we share. Due to the volume of IV fluid they give us, we rustle past the curtain often. We both need to piss into a plastic, juice-style pitcher with volume measurements down the side. I have mine; he has his. There's a checklist: note the volume, pour the urine into the toilet, cover the toilet with a plastic shield, flush the toilet, write the volume on a sheet on the inside of the bathroom door. The flush shield is to protect the janitors who clean these bone marrow–ward bathrooms from being exposed to aerosolized chemotherapy coming out of the toilet into the air. The nurses are very concerned that I measure each day's urine. I was not told about this beforehand. I'm on IV fluids twenty-four hours a day to keep my kidneys going as they pump this scorched-earth chemotherapy into me, so I guess it makes sense. If there's a disparity between the volume coming in through the IV and the volume going out in my urine, where is the difference? I assume it would be in my lungs or something awful, but don't actually know.

My roommate has a sheet of his own on the inside of the bathroom door, showing his numbers. My numbers are higher, are better. It's not a contest, of course. Obviously.

We don't talk, he and I. I don't know his name. He's told me his name, I'm sure, but I don't know it. We keep our urine pitchers on the back of the toilet, and they are labelled so we don't confuse them, but I still don't know his name. Maybe his name is George.

Days pass and the chemo goes into me and then stops, and we begin to wait for things to get awful. George's buddy comes to visit. I listen to their conversation through the curtain. They talk about cars. Mercedes Benz. BMW. Audi. About which car is the best.

And boats. And golfing. George wants to golf again, drive nice cars again. The buddy is all support, fast talking, agitated. George has some nasty kind of leukemia, I've deduced. The leukemia may be in and around his spinal cord, which is not where you want it. Lots of leukemias up here on the fifteenth floor. Up to now, I've been of the opinion that leukemias are mild and get zapped no problem, but that's probably not true. He's a few weeks beyond the bone marrow transplant, ahead of me, on the mend. Feeling good. But they are keeping him here, not letting him leave, though he wants to leave. He talks with the buddy about how soon he can leave — very soon, they've told him, they've promised — and how great it will be to get out. Yeah, says the buddy, yeah, yeah, yeah, yeah, yeah.

A few days later, the head oncologist comes into the room and closes the curtain to speak with George in private. The doctor talks about how, yes, he knows they said *things* were looking good, but now they aren't looking so good.

"What?" asks George.

"The things," says the doctor. "They aren't looking so good."

George doesn't understand. Did the head oncologist not say at an earlier date that things were looking good? He did, says the head oncologist, he did say that things were looking good, at that earlier date. But now. Yes, but now. Some stuff going on around the spine. Some stuff going on inside the bones. I don't catch everything. I'm on drugs, woozy, starting my long descent through ablation and cell death, though I don't yet feel them fully, don't yet comprehend the scope. Anyway, now they can't let George leave, cannot discharge him as they said they would. He isn't happy. Because they said he could go on a particular date and now the date has changed. Almost everything that happens to people on this ward is chiselled and set in stone, but the dates are not.

It will be more chemo for George. Just a little more. To get more of the cancer. To scour away the stuff bothering these doctors. And then they will discharge him, at that later date. They will? Yes, they will see how these new injections go, and then at that later date possibly discharge. How does that sound? Okay, okay.

Later, George's wife visits. He's upset. She's sad or angry, had also grown attached to the now-cancelled discharge date. They are cold to each other. Marriage must be hard. With the devastation. With the kids. And she's sitting in a chair at the foot of the bed — I can hear its legs squeak against the hard plastic floor — and trying to say that it'll all work out. Interesting that she's in a chair. There is no sitting on the edge of his bed, no cuddling. But then again, I don't know, maybe old people don't cuddle. Maybe they aren't together anymore. Maybe it's just the kids they have, if they have kids. Just the duty to be present, as dates change.

I have my own dates to consider. No discharge set for me. Much too early. Far to go before that is even considered. First, these drugs taking hold and killing off every white blood cell. When they are all dead, I will rebuild an immune system so this never happens again. But I try not to hope for that, try not to feel it's promised, though how I'm feeling now makes such promises seem owed for having to go through such misery. A new immune system. What an idea. Not fully new, though. The same scaffold, the same code of *me*. And the promises? I won't get them, and George won't get them — they are not ours. Instead, we'll both just be in this cold room, on our sides of the curtain, listening to each other's lives and drawing our conclusions.

•

EVERY OTHER DAY, I GO TO THE YMCA to work out. The building, like me, is old and broken down, but I love it there. How the gate dings as I swipe my card to get in and a small LED glows green and I know exactly what will happen next, what exercises

I'll do, how I'll feel doing them. Some day soon this place will get demolished. The ceilings are a maze of exposed piping and ducts and captured asbestos. Built in the seventies and painted beige, it's full of mixed-use rooms and ancient pulley machines. But it's a good gym, a gym of people working *at something.* Victoria's winter is damp and cold, even without much snow or many sub-zero temperatures. The chill gets to me. And after I've been working in the freezers and fridges at the deli all day, after waiting for the bus out in the rain, this gym feels like the only warm place in the world. When I go there, I *know* I'll be warm, no matter what, warmer than in my apartment, warmer than in the shower.

If I close the deli at nine, I can just make it for a workout before the gym closes at ten thirty. After a while, I recognize almost everyone. The old guys on testosterone. The Instagram girls. The young guys with disconcerting Band-Aids on their upper thighs, the back acne. Always the same people. They must recognize me, too, the other patrons, though perhaps not in a good way. I must be the worst regular of them all. The least strong. I'm the guy never using a program, the guy lifting until I'm tired. Such an approach does work, to an extent, but I don't make rapid progress. Being able to lift a specific number is not my top priority. I go for the warmth. I go for the feeling of afterward. I go for some respite from the internal voices and to be around people without having to talk to them.

I stick to an every-other-day routine for years. I just go every other day. Not a complex rule. And I stick to it even though I keep getting injured. There's something wrong with me. Not in the sense of having-cancer wrong, but like my body does not function well. My muscles are so tight at rest that even basic movements hurt or lead to injury. Massage, physio, doctors, stretching, yoga, foam rolling, trigger points, acupuncture, intramuscular stimulation — I try it all. It takes me years to even realize that what's happening in my body is not physical. At some point the body gets stuck in one mode, a mode of being in danger, and that mode never turns off. That's really what it is. But at the same time, that's *really* what it is. There are many types of fear, and each type controls us in different ways. For a while I don't clue into what's going on and rationalize that I have various diseases. But there are no diseases, or at least none of the diseases I imagine. The fantasies of my dying persist, though. Being in that palliative bed as people trundle past saying their goodbyes. My body wants to fight this danger that cannot be fought. I should get therapy, but don't.

Whenever an appointment with my oncologist looms, I hit the workouts harder. Even as my joints swell and ache trying to work through the muscle tightness that will not go away, I push so hard before those appointments. Shoulder pain especially. I just cannot progress on bench press without my shoulders hurting so much that I can't use my computer or close my fist. Some days, trying to grip slices of ham with the deli tongs, I can hardly squeeze them together, trembling. I don't tell anyone, and there are no sick days for rest anyway. But I *still* keep working out. Every other day is the rule. I cannot break the rule.

There's something about having to go to the cancer centre. Of their having this big file on me. I want to be in the best shape possible for the encounter. I want to walk like an Olympian into the building that has taken so much from me. I want the doctor to say I will be okay based only on my appearance, on if I'm vascular, on how my clavicles look. It's so dumb. I do it every time. When they do their lymph node exam, I'm like, "I can take off my shirt. It's not a big deal." There's always some internal monologue of *You know all those other patients of yours who died and got ugly? Not me*. It's so fucking dumb. I should stop.

It's important to work out on cancer-appointment day. Two hours before is ideal. This way you still have a good pump going when they see you. Try to be vascular, especially the upper body.

Hit the bench, rows, curls, that kind of stuff. And when the doctor asks if I'm keeping active, I say, "Here and there," and shrug, like I'm just built different. The funny part is, I'm not even that fit, so the entire process only exists in my head. Physical medicines change as I get older and leapfrog from treatment to treatment, but the other purer medicines like theatrics and delusion remain the same.

•

IT STARTED WITH VITAMIN D, as I'm from Yukon and have never known sunlight. Taking one vitamin D pill a day in the aftermath of that first cancer felt like a step in the right direction. I was in my early twenties, after all, and needed to be serious about my health. I sometimes missed days, but even sporadic pills at the base of my tongue felt like a measure of control. What else was I going to do? Become a vegetarian? In the beginning, I kept it simple: vitamins D, B, C, even E if feeling off-kilter or fuzzy. These were the days before I knew the word *stack*, as in *my stack of pills*, the mélange of daily tablets that promises to keep me safe and strong and virile and mentally razor sharp. After the basic vitamins of, like, *being alive*, you can always go further, if you think it's important. There is a lot out there to put in your body.

What happens is, you take these vitamins every day for a while and don't die, so you start to think, *Hey these are fine and important. I need to keep taking these.* So you do. Then, when you forget your vitamins on a trip or run out and the pharmacy is closed, you get worried about this sudden dangerous situation of not having your little white tablets every morning, as if they make all the difference. And whenever the cancer comes back, that's a sign you haven't been doing enough. You could have done more but didn't, and now it's back with the chemotherapy and the misery, all because you were too lazy to really do the research, to really be diligent.

After second cancer, with my anxiety levels so high I'm barely functioning, I look into more things I could take. Ashwagandha comes up in those first searches, a kind of "adaptogen" plant that people — online dudes with profile pictures of anime girls, I mean — speak glowingly about. Really, it's just Indian ginseng or winter cherry and has been around in Ayurveda forever. The ashwagandha is expensive and takes nine weeks to arrive from India, which further convinces me of its effectiveness. I'm excited. This could be the thing that makes the panic attacks go away. That would be amazing. The order arrives in a bubble-wrapped cylinder. I cut it open with scissors, pop a few of the bubbles for fun, then eat a small spoonful of the beige powder. I'm hyper for hours and don't sleep well. The flavour, too, suffers from a bitter, fang-like aftertaste. But there's a feeling in my body after taking it. Something happens. If it's good or bad, I don't know. One thing the ashwagandha doesn't do is let me have sex ten times a day, which seemed to be indicated by what the dudes said online, though I don't get a chance to make sure. But that's okay. There are always other things.

From there I discover maca root, a tuber that Peruvians and other South Americans have been using for miscellaneous sex reasons for millennia. This substance doesn't seem to have anticancer claims, but it arrives as a big plastic bag of brown powder without any labelling, which, again, gives it an air of seriousness. The maca is also expensive and also takes nine weeks to arrive, but this is my health and wellness at stake. I need to be more serious. I'm already preparing myself to be healthy and aggressively energized and able to have sex ten times a day. With the maca I just plug my nose and swallow some. This leads to a lot of stomach pain, and yes, energy, but it makes me feel weird, so I put it in the cupboard and never try it again.

I stick with zinc, too. It's fine to take zinc, *might actually* also make your dick better, and as long as I'm not hungover and take it with food, it doesn't hurt too much.

Magnesium is the next stab at the anxiety. There's some research on magnesium, though it also hurts my stomach and makes me almost shit my pants. But that's okay. There's always something else. Between these forays, I'm eating raw garlic and ginger by the spoonful, the garlic for immune support and fighting off colds, the ginger for clearing my sinuses and making me feel warm all over.

Eventually, I find a different kind of magnesium made by this dubiously qualified lady in New York. This scientific magnesium will supposedly *not* make me shit my pants, but still offers the same soothing benefits. The very first time I try this special atomic magnesium, which is almost stupidly expensive, I do feel more relaxed, but every time afterward I don't feel anything. Also my sleep worsens, which is the opposite of what magnesium is supposed to do. Is this because of the atomic magnesium or because of my crumbling mental health? I don't know. How can you know? Stacks move and shift and it's hard to be certain how one part of your stack might interact with another. Then again, there's the protein isolate, that one's fine, and the creatine, which I don't take long-term, though it also has good research.

I begin to dabble again, vitamin D, C, zinc, ginger, lots of ginger, maybe too much ginger, and even weird shit like lemon balm, apple cider vinegar, whatever might give me an edge. Anything for that edge. Like, what I put in my body must matter, right? That's the feeling. The feeling of helplessness. That if you have any control, which you must, logically, you need to do the utmost. To not be killed by the next cancer. No matter how much it costs or how much you are in pain or even whether it's safe. Keep going, don't stop. And when doctors ask you if you are taking any medication, say no, and be telling the truth.

I GET MY FIRST STORY published at twenty-nine. It's picked up by the *Malahat Review*, a publication I've been trying to get into for years. The story took three years to write, which is much too long. Do not spend this long on a story. I'd work on it and work on it, never sending it anywhere, only really realizing what it was about while elbow-deep in a sink of chicken grease at work. The story is about a mom whose only son becomes an enlightened Buddha and obtains magical powers when he's eight years old. Other kids ostracize him. His mom can't cope with his withdrawal into meditation. She tries everything to get him back to normal, but nothing works. Her son is gone to her, she feels. The mom is also dealing with a pile of body-image issues, and her marriage, and there's a whole arc that I cut from the final draft where she's attracted to the giant muscular women at her gym. I write a bunch of endings.

The first scrapped ending has the family take their boat out on the ocean for a picnic. The mom, dad, and Buddha son cruising through the waves with a blue sky overhead, trying to reclaim what was lost. Far out to sea, they come across another boat. It's kind of like their boat, but empty. There is evidence that another family was in the boat: torn sandwich bags, soda cans lolling in the tilt of the waves, a tipped-over cooler. What has happened to the other family? And so the mom and dad board this other boat among all the menace, and then the Buddha son leaps into the ocean and starts swimming for shore, though it's miles off. Then the mom jumps in the water and swims after the son, pulls alongside, and they start swim racing.

The other ending focuses on a homoerotic Buddhist situation between the son and his best friend that involves him almost getting beaten to death in a fit of passionate rage.

In the real ending, the ending that gets published, the son begins to meditate under a tree in the yard and ceases communicating with his parents. They try and get him to engage, to speak to them, but he remains mute. Soon, monks from a nearby Buddhist temple come to pray with the son, to worship, and on the fourth night the son disappears and doesn't return.

•

IT'S STRANGE TO SIT AT the head of the table in the same class-room I took my first workshop in as a student. The students wait for me to say something, and I try to focus. I still haven't published a story, I'm such a fraud. They must be wondering *Who is this man? He's so young*. Must be very good, to be young and teaching. Accomplished. An awful feeling. The last time I was in this building was for my thesis defence in the two weeks between the awful GDP chemotherapy and the soon-to-come and even more awful stem cell transplant chemotherapy. It was in one of the other small workshop classrooms, my mentors all on the committee. Some students watching me do a reading, a girl I had a major crush on there, too. Sweating through my shirts, trying to not shake. Also mostly bald and still swollen from the extreme prednisone doses, but I pulled through okay.

The students in this class are mostly women, as usual, some not old enough to drink, some my age, some older. I don't know what I talk about that first day. Maybe the syllabus. Maybe about what's *important*. My hands tremble. Still not fully recovered from the stem cell transplant. Not really. Maybe never. Hoping I at least look normal now that my hair is back. They cannot tell what happened; it's fine. I give them a reading list of writers I like, which is mostly the writers my teachers liked. I am such a cliché.

Seeing the students with their notebooks and binders, I think of *my* second year, in the same classroom. I had Lorna Jackson, who was incredible and driven and divisive. So many students afraid of her, how she locked the door when the class started, and failed people, and someone always cried, and students crucified her in the ratemyprofessors.com reviews. How much of it is true, I don't know; she was always fair to me, though I like adversity and being told no, or maybe just fucking hate being told no so much that I'll do whatever it takes to not have it happen again. Those first stories I submitted to her make me smile now, how bad they were. I'd never really written anything before and she gave me Cs, saying I needed to learn how grammar worked if I wanted good grades. Commas at that point meant almost nothing to me, how to write a sentence somehow not part of my education. Though whether that's ever changed, I don't know. My only advantage going into her class was having read like only the bullied do for the previous ten years.

Over the next weeks, we fall into the typical rhythms of workshop. Stories come in one week, are discussed the next. The students span a range. Some still having their characters awaken from a dream at the end. One so brilliant it's almost pointless to have her in the workshop at all — she should be skipped ahead, if possible, or banished and told to go out into the world. There was no one this good back in my student days. I tell her in my written comments to pursue writing or art or whatever, to go beyond this little class. Such sage advice. Hilarious. Why would she listen to me? Or I could tell her that being good isn't enough. That being smart isn't enough. That you need to also be stupid, so stupid you won't give up in the face of failure and poverty and rejection, so stupid you accept that even succeeding will not be successful. I can't tell yet if she's stupid in this way, and maybe she doesn't care that much to begin with. She doesn't owe the world her talent.

I get more comfortable teaching but am still not being simple enough. Whenever I think I've explained the fundament of something, I realize I haven't. I have to keep going back, keep unfolding the complications until it is all a flat piece of paper. How-to-write books pose the same questions — *What is their motivation? What do they want? What are the stakes?* — but these are way too complex. Such questions are too easy to ask. No, you need to go back. Instead, write a sentence like *There is a stone on the ground.* Even that might be too complex. How about *A stone?* That can be your sentence. Let me see the stone. Let me see a cat. If you can do that, you can do anything.

•

IT'S FRIDAY AND MY LONG-TIME buddy invites me over for a drink before we go down to the pool hall. This buddy doesn't have his own place in town and has been staying on another friend's couch. He's inviting me to the friend's place. We all know each other, so I assume it's fine. He sends the invite over text. The apartment is only a few blocks away, so I throw on my good blue sweater and head out. It's fall and the trees are bare and jagged, and a cutting wind whips up Yates Street from the harbour with the smell of dead leaves and salt.

When I arrive, the buddy is sitting on the couch/his bed, drunk. Okay, well, it's not weird for him to be drunk, but I now grasp that he is drunker than his text message implied. I go into the kitchen and sit at the table. The kitchen has a lot of cream linoleum, as my family's kitchen did when I was a kid. The friend whose place this is walks by, looking pissed. He says hi then goes into his room and closes the door. The wasted friend sways into the kitchen and takes a seat. Where is the other friend's sister? Doesn't she live here too? I then remember hearing that couch-buddy has been perhaps sleeping with the sister. He keeps talking at me. I don't feel well. Whatever is going on here twists through my stomach. I hear crying down the hall — the sister. I grab a beer from the fridge as the wasted buddy talks. He's not making sense. Loud. Referencing the stupid friend who won't come out of his room, like a baby, and saying that the crying sister is not a big deal and that everything is fine.

We drink a few more beers, though this buddy should be having zero more beers. He's drunk enough that his eyes are closed all the way now, no longer squinted — he is only seeing the blue-grey of eyelids, the orange pulse of the kitchen lights on the other side. When I'm that drunk, closing my eyes makes me dizzy. I'm not often that drunk anymore.

The sober friend periodically comes out of his room to grab water or an apple, then goes back in and closes the door. He's still pissed off — rightly, I'm sure. I think he's playing a video game; I hear the mouse clicks. The sister has not shown herself, and I don't ask.

There's a knock at the front door. Who could it be? Ah, it's the sober friend's parents. They, too, have come to drink beer. I'm sweating so much. The father sits at the table next to the shut-eyed friend. He seems to be content with the drunkenness level. Is the father also drunk? When I was growing up, my parents almost never drank in front of me, so when I see it now, it unnerves me. The wasted friend and the father begin to converse and argue, and the friend is getting very loud and sometimes yelling, eyes still closed. I'm saying absolutely nothing. The sister is still in her room, but no longer crying loud enough for me to hear. He really shouldn't be sleeping with the sister. That's not okay when on the couch.

The beers I'm swallowing aren't enough to hold back the bad feeling in my stomach and at the back of my teeth. After another hour of this, with the drunk friend now ranting incomprehensibly, I get up, say bye to the friend who's in his room playing the game, and walk home. I make sure my apartment door is locked and sit at my desk staring at the black computer screen. What is happening to me?

I stay inside the next four days, eating whatever food I have on hand. Oatmeal. Cereal. Frozen chicken. I've never not wanted to go outside in this way before, but it doesn't seem safe, so I stay in the apartment. I start meditating on day two and start taking leftover cancer-Ativan on day three, which makes me feel quite a bit better and lets me sleep. As the days trickle by, the doom feeling wanes, and on the fifth day I go to the grocery store for supplies. I haven't been answering the drunk friend's messages and am not sure I will again.

•

I'M ASLEEP IN MY CHILDHOOD room when the phone wakes me up. Calls at this hour, I know who it is, but I ask anyway because I'm on vacation and demand clarity. There's mucus at the corner of my eye that will not let go, but I say I'm awake, say this is a good time. The hematologist from Vancouver, of course. We do our introductions. She's overseen my case for years, though I've only met her once, years back at her office in Vancouver before the stem cell transplant. But now that the cancer is back again, here she is. What's up? I'm starting to get the feeling doctors don't know what to do with me.

She asks how I've been. Asks how I feel about the diagnosis. I'm remembering being a kid in this room, all the things I had yet to know. Remembering the scent of wood smoke, that one night with my high school girlfriend, the constant light in the summer with towels on the windows, the mosquitoes and their blood splatters, the clouds of weed smoke with my brother. The doctor and I start talking options. She shapes each word with care, faint English accent, not wanting any confusion. What do I think of another stem cell transplant? Allogeneic this time, someone else's cells. Lots of danger with allogeneic. I don't know what to say. What do I think?

What is my opinion? Some situations only pretend to be choices and it's important to identify them immediately. I wonder if they even know what to do. Maybe a treatment *has* to be offered as a choice if it might boil me in an incendiary immune reaction. A person should have to choose. No doctor wants to compel that, right?

She is going to bring my case up with the lymphoma tribunal or whatever — I always picture a table of wizards. So rare, this cancer. So tricky. She circles back to the transplant idea. I try not to remember the other one, its brutality. And this one would be worse, much worse. Yes, yes, she says, there are risks. Because it's the morning, I just ask her: what is the likelihood of this maybe fatal transplant curing me?

There's a pause. "Well, I would say … sixty percent. I would say sixty percent chance of a cure."

I think about that. Our breathing on the phone line, the silence, the sound. Sixty percent. Maybe that's good. Maybe that's bad. And what's left from a hundred is forty. Forty percent being that I relapse again and again like I already do. Forty percent being an abbreviated lifetime of graft-versus-host disease. Forty percent being death. Which is it? So much math. So much to consider. And we say goodbye, and I don't know what to do or choose.

Later that month she calls again to say the transplant is off the table. They don't want to fire that bullet yet. For now, keep it chambered. Still aimed at me with a little laser beam on my heart, yes, certainly, but unfired. More chemo is the new plan. I'll find out which variety later. This one might work better. Might be the one. Doubtful now. Too often expecting and being let down. Better to form a kind of holding pattern over doom, airborne and gliding and never quite getting away.

•

SHE'S IN BED ON HER stomach, binder open across my pillow, analyzing a hand-drawn picture of a heart. The binder is thick and has colour-coded dividers. My binders at school always looked like shit, pages half-torn-out, bent rings, marker doodles of explosions on the cover. She asks whether I care if she studies. I say no. All the components of the heart are labelled, and there are more than I remember. What is a tricuspid? She says her program includes a complete anatomy class, that massage can interact with certain prescription drugs, that things are all incorporated. I kiss her shoulder. Back when we were in workshop all those years ago writing poetry, I should have asked her out. The one poem she submitted, about a snow leopard, how it's like a teacup, is probably still on my computer. Every damn thing from back then still on there. Those workshops. Such a crush on her. The measured way she'd talk. And now, eight years later, this *thing* we're doing. Three years ago, right before the stem cell transplant, she got coffee with me a few times. Unclear if those were dates or she felt bad or what. At the time, I was not doing well, right in the thick of the extreme chemo they give before the stem cell chemo. I'm sure she could tell I was not doing well. She's perceptive. But now I'm okay. Now, I'm okay.

She only wears dresses and always has her hair up. We look absurd walking together, me almost a foot and a half taller. I don't give a shit. She gives me spontaneous hour-long massages, real massages, asking me where it hurts. Where would I even say? How would I specify? I do not know how to acknowledge this level of care. I give her less-good massages of my own and pretend like I'm not trying to be a real massage therapist, but I'm sure she can tell.

Her binder on the pillow is so full of paper. Endless information on how to touch. She even read the unpublished novel I've given up on. Said she loved it. What is wrong with her? I'm only human, can only withstand so much. Stress locks my body into rigid shapes, and she'll run her hands up my back, pointing out how tight this or that is, that some parts appear to be missing. Sometimes she'll ask me to traction her lower back. She's got an SI joint injury. I don't know what the SI joint is, but hers is injured, and I am here. So, as she lies on her stomach, I'll straddle her legs, put my hands on each side of her bottom ribs, and push up, gently, holding. How her whole body lengthens when I do this. And then she'll sigh, her scapula drooping. I am so skilled. I have so much potential. And then we'll watch movies, and then I'll make popcorn, and then it'll be dark.

III

STAGE 3A

lymph node involvement:
above and below diaphragm;
groin; near aorta

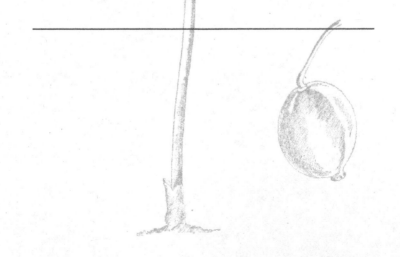

✤

WHEN IT COMES BACK, THERE'S comfort, even peace — I recognize that now. Here again, no longer having to worry about the worst possible thing. Cancer, the third. Enter a sequence of known events. Imaging comes first, the radioactive juice wheeled over on its lead-armoured cart, the cart looking higher tech than last time. They take their pictures, and someone very educated holds the pictures up to a bright light. There will be surgery. There's always surgery, in one way or another. Then blood tests, endless blood tests. Some veins with so much scar tissue they can't be used anymore. I'll be given a schedule for infusions, the calendar with bright green numbers on the already terrifying days. People are mobilized. Top minds. Everything taken care of.

Go on sick leave from washing dishes at the university, max that out, then special leave, maybe even try for leave pooled from co-workers if there is any. Quit the job. Sure. Impossible to work. Can't do it. Not in a million years. Hear about people doing it, working through to support family, driven by a system that leaves no choice. Friends reach out, tentative. Or if I see them, it comes up. They don't know how many times it's been at this point, but that's okay. Who can keep track? It's a lot. It's too much. People send cards with images of kittens or blue shorelines or deep cedar forests. I'm blown away by the things written inside and think, *Do they love me?* I can never write anything interesting or profound in cards, even though that feels crucial. Sometimes just signing a name. Draw a smiley. Draw a picture of a heart. What do you put in a card? I stuff the cards into the bookshelf next to my extra pairs of glasses and a paper-wrapped pouch of LSD and a deck of playing cards from Japan.

The bad has arrived. Breathe. And it is bad, yes, very bad. This time might be the final time — it must come eventually. Sit inside for days. Skip workouts. Eat old crackers and canned fruit. When it comes back, it's like someone who promised to pick you up from somewhere in their car, somewhere you want away from, and they don't show, and it hurts and is a betrayal, but eventually they are there, an outline beyond the distortion of the windshield, and you know who it is, know their ridges and soft points, can tell from afar.

●

WE ARRIVE IN JAPAN AT some o'clock in the morning. I took an Ativan during the flight and lost track of things, but I'm back now, smelling the Tokyo airport's concrete aroma. Our cousin Jon is getting married, so here we are, the whole family minus Jess, who's back in Yukon, too pregnant to travel. What a massive, orderly airport. Eventually, we make it to the street, where hot rain falls sideways on us, but it's good to be outside again, good to know there is an outside. It's been two weeks since the doctor sat me in his little orange examination room and told me the cancer was back. The family, these tired people staring at the skyscrapers, are doing a good job not bringing it up. I'm sure the cousins know, too.

Maybe everyone knows. Feels like *I'm* the only one who doesn't know — the data is there, cancer in my body, above and below the diaphragm, but it still feels like the third person.

Rain on my glasses smears the city into neon impressionism. We look for taxis but are on the wrong side of the road, of course. When we do get a taxi, the driver looks us over — we are all giants — and looks worried and flips open his phone to call a second taxi, perhaps a third. Billboards and glass coat the skyline. Electrical wires criss-cross the roads like ribbons. There is no trash anywhere. The fleet of cabs drops us off at the hotel in Ginza, which must be the expensive part of the city because the black suits are tighter and all the women wear tan trench coats. On the street, countless umbrellas fly past at eyeball height, and we stumble half-asleep into the hotel and crash out.

I've never travelled with the family like this outside of Canada. The McDonald's here is very good, each breakfast McMuffin perfectly crafted, fresh from an advertisement. I feel lame eating McDonald's but haven't quite figured out what I should be eating. I'm already thinking of chemo, what it will do to my stomach. The bride's family is really going all out with tours and getting us on buses and showing us temples and castles and imperial koi ponds. I try to say thank you when I can. *Arigato, arigato.*

A lot of the food has eyeballs. I'll think it's a deep-fried piece of onion, but then it will have an eyeball. At the roadside stores, you can buy bottles of minnows in slime, and we all come over to look at them. Maybe my palate sucks. The ramen is incredible, the broth, the noodles. We are using restaurant apps. Going to the good places. While we're still in Tokyo, my younger brother, Alex, suggests we check out a place called Sukiyabashi Jiro that's nearby in the subway, says it has good reviews on Yelp. I ask if it's the

Sukiyabashi Jiro that's the best sushi restaurant in the world, with three Michelin stars, because I'm being an asshole. We don't go.

My parents keep eating at McDonald's. Maybe we are all eating too much McDonald's. Outside Kyoto we are taken to this immaculate Zen-garden dining house, the whole thing rented for the extended family. We dine kneeling — for about one minute before everyone has to switch to sitting cross-legged — on tatami in front of tiny wooden place settings. Waitresses in kimonos shuffle on their knees with a many-course meal of small servings arranged on darkly coloured ceramic dishes. Anna, my cousin, is pregnant and skipping lots of the food. I'm transfixed by the rain falling onto the garden. My appetite's gone, so I turn around to make watching the garden easier. The greenness is so intense I have to blink. Moss-covered stones. Ponds with lily pads. What am I going to do this time? The treatment will be worse than all the other times, I suspect. No girlfriend, at least; that would be complicated. And now with the summer lay-off from dishwashing, ample free time to dread and collect myself.

The wedding is in Gifu, a small town in the outskirts of Nagoya, at a mixed indoor-outdoor event centre. A *Shintō* ceremony comes first, with Jon in *hakama* and Eri in a cream cowl with wood slippers, as monks drone and hum. Lots of stuff is said in Japanese. Then they have us all gather below the balcony outside, and either wedding staff or friends of the family begin to throw towels into the crowd. Eri's family owns a towel company. I'm below the balcony as the towels rain down, a foot taller than everyone not in my family, snatching *many* towels out of the grasping hands of old Japanese ladies. Alex must not be focused because he ends up empty-handed even though he's taller than me. I give him a purple towel to balance my karma. Then they are throwing candy and trinkets, but I let the old Japanese ladies have their fill. These towels are lovely and soft and much too small to be useful, but I still want all of them.

Once we transition to the dinner hall, I end up at the same table as my brother and one of my cousins on my mother's side. The venue is all white tablecloths, fine cutlery, and a little squid in a martini glass for the first course. Alex drinks my squid for me. Part of me thinks I shouldn't have come here, to Japan, but the flights were already booked. You don't not go to Japan. I've got my blue suit on, red tie. I look good, even if I'm sweating like crazy. The suit jacket holds in most of the sweat, and so long as I wipe my brow, no one will realize.

I haven't slept much. At night, I stare into the blinking lights of the hotel's alarm clock, thinking, *It's just the jetlag. You aren't devastated.* I drape a book over the alarm clock, a shirt over the microwave's neon screen, a sock over the air conditioner, anything to darken the room enough for me to be blind.

The bride and groom have disappeared.

Suddenly, music! Metal guitars! And Jon's brothers, Pete and Benji, come out in white karate *gi* with topknot wigs on. Pete told me they were doing this, but to see it is amazing. Both have wooden *katana*, and as the music continues, they pace around menacingly, holding the swords overhead and pointing them at various guests like they might be next. Then a shift in the music, the drums hit, and Jon descends the big staircase in black *hakama* with a *katana* of his own — his topknot is real; he grew it out for the wedding. He attacks his two evil brothers. The music switches to Al Hirt's "Green Hornet" from *Kill Bill*, the swords clash, and first Benji, then Pete, are slain.

Everyone goes wild.

But where is Eri? Where is the bride?

Only now do I notice a large white fabric globe in the courtyard, beyond the sliding doors of the reception hall. Jon approaches the globe, *katana* held high, and slashes down. The gauzy material parts and falls to the ground, and there is Eri in her *Shintō* gown and cowl and high-soled slippers. He leads her to safety as we all clap and cheer.

And then we're eating and eating. I'm not really eating, but I'm drinking the beers they keep bringing me. I see my uncle over at another table explaining to the servers that he's allergic to the shellfish. They nod and bow and smile warmly and shuffle off. Twenty minutes later the chef personally comes out and gives him a plate with a big lobster on it, to make sure all is well.

A film crew documents everything. There are multiple cameras, cords everywhere. A woman in a black pantsuit crawls on the floor behind Eri at certain points to make sure her dress trails properly. When next the bride and groom appear, Eri's wearing an all-white dress that looks like ocean froth. Jon's in a silver swallow-tail suit, like a supervillain fresh off a hot-air balloon.

And we eat more — those of us eating — and drink, and then she's feeding Jon from the cake with a spoon the size of a shovel. They switch outfits again, she in a gold dress, he in black, then again, she in a rainbow princess-style dress with so many layers I can't count them as they shift and move. Someone is talking about how in Japan they rent ten-thousand-dollar dresses for weddings, but who knows — I'm near drunk and the energy is just right. Before we leave the dinner hall, the film crew shows the film of the wedding to us. I can't believe it. They've already made the film? Somehow, I don't know how, they edited together the most intense moments, added music, and arranged everything into a five-minute film. And so we all watch the marriage film of the marriage we've just attended, and it's quite touching and tastefully shot.

We transition back to the hotel for the after-party at the local karaoke spot. I love the karaoke spot. You can bring in your own alcohol and snacks. Each room has, like, seven microphones, digital drum sets, cushioned benches along the walls. Everyone is singing. I do "Forgot About Dre," then we do some from *Aladdin* and *The Emperor's New Groove*, the classics, the important ones like "One Jump Ahead." People are getting a bit wild. In the other room, Eri's family is singing, but I don't go in because it seems very serious, each person taking their specific turn, no rapping, while everyone else quietly observes and claps at the end. In our room we howl and bang on the walls. Someone is slamming plastic sticks against the digital drum set that isn't even plugged in. People argue about what song to play. People go out to get more beer and then come back, and we all prepare to keep going.

Two days after the ceremony, my sister and I take the bullet train to Hiroshima. We are in Japan after all, and it feels necessary. Angela's got better hot-weather clothing than me. I don't even have shorts. The humidity climbs as our train tears across the countryside, the only sense of speed a quiet humming at the base of my neck. I can't feel the humidity inside the train, but I can see it beyond the windows, the lush wall of forest, the dew-filled warp to the air. I'm thinking it will be nice to have my small cancer-having problems overshadowed by what happened at our destination.

Once we step into the city proper, the swelter hits. Air saturated beyond anything I've felt before. We walk a few blocks from the train station to the atomic memorial, then across a wide stone bridge over the Motoyasu River's grey-blue water. The park bustles with people. Tourists. Guides. Crowds of school children walking from monument to monument, all holding hands. Near the water, there's a pagoda with vines stitched through its latticework roof. I sit in the shade on a wooden bench, staring up at the little rays of light that peek through the leaves. I'm hot. I'm tired. But there is so much to see. Ang is motivated.

We head inside the museum building and look at displayed items found within the blast radius. Melted tricycles that look like large paper clips. Blackened rags. Ash imprints. The photographs of the aftermath, people's skin falling off in sheets, the obliterated world. I don't stay in the exhibits for long.

As we leave to explore different areas outside, a group of kids shyly approaches us. We are Canadians, yes? They have questions for a school assignment.

"Okay," we say. "Ask away."

One of them steps forward and asks us whether, seeing this place, seeing what happened here, we still believe in love?

"Yes," I say. "Yes, I do believe."

"Good," he says. They all grin. Then they ask Ang. She says yes, too. The children scribble our answers in their notebooks and thank us for our time. And soon, we're walking back to the train station, sunburned and hungover still, not really talking about it, not really sure if there's anything left to discuss or see, though there always is.

•

A JANUARY STORM HISSES AGAINST the windows. There isn't much space to sit in my apartment, so we're in bed. Light from the desk lamp paints her shoulder, this new woman, Ronnie, I like very much. Black hair keeps getting in my mouth. I'm looking at a cobweb near the window, one arm draped over her waist, thinking I should have cleaned it. Didn't see the cobweb, distracted, scared to tell her.

There's something she needs to know. What is it? Expectant at first — a gift? Then seeing my face. We've only known each other two months. Such a short time for this. What does a person think when the one they're in bed with says they need to know something? So many terrible possibilities. Understanding this, I say, no, no, it's nothing *bad*. Only that, things will be *difficult* for the next while. For me. Very difficult. And if she doesn't want to be a part of these coming realities, it's okay, I understand. We are just beginning, after all. Still time for her to get out. I tell her the rest, but still lie about how many times I've had cancer, fudge those numbers a bit, still not ready.

She's looking at the ceiling. I can't meet her eyes. Five months for the treatment? You'll be very sick? Sick, yes, and bald. Maybe hospitalized. I won't be able to see her in the days after infusions, won't want to see her. Will you die? No, no, no. Probably not. Of course not. My organs older now. Thirties. Liver pain, kidney. Well, I haven't died yet. Not last time, or the time before that. She runs a hand through my hair, inspecting. Bald? You'll look good. I'll make you soup. And that she says is enough.

•

I WAKE IN THE MIDDLE of the night to the sound of heavy rain. But no. No. The glow through the curtains red, the sound not of drops. A savage crackling. I crawl from bed and peek out my apartment's cobwebbed window. The Dumpster next to the building is on fire. Engulfed. The fence around the Dumpster also alight. Not that far from the building, this fire. And the building's electrical transformer box snuggled right against that fence. Smoke in a cyclone. There are other partially clothed people at other dark apartment windows, their faces lit red. Someone should do something.

Our building is only one block from the fire department. Soon, the big yellow truck arrives and the firefighters, all geared up, blast the conflagration with water. Plumes of vapour and smoke fill the night air. Drops spatter the window, now sounding like real rain. I just stand at the window in my underwear, stomach all wound up. Fires always take longer to put out than you'd think. The Dumpster still aglow in the torrent, like a sunken eye. Then dimmer. Dimmer still. These firefighters are smart, they know to give no quarter when extinguishing — something I never learned. All of us standing at our windows, leaning slightly away from everything. Water runs in rivers across the parking lot and collects in dark ponds at its lowest points. The blackened lattice of the fence caves in. Cars shine in the fire truck's headlights. All the cars are silver. The Dumpster now jagged and impartial. I go back to sleep.

The next day, I see the thick-denimed building manager standing in the parking lot, his thumbs in belt loops, observing the wreckage. "What happened?" I ask.

"Oh," he says. "Well, there's this guy who goes around arsoning Dumpsters, so that's my theory as to what happened. Been doing it for a while."

"A guy?"

"Yeah, a guy who arsons Dumpsters. It's his thing."

"He's done this to other Dumpsters around town?"

"Oh yeah, tons."

"That could go bad," I say.

"Yeah."

"But it hasn't yet?"

"Not yet."

•

MY SISTER ANG AND HER best friend, Helena, strategize a weekend getaway for me between chemo treatments. My mom's in on it, paying, I bet, always so generous. We'll be staying on the bottom floor of an oceanfront mansion near Jordan River, this remote place a few hours up Vancouver Island from Victoria. On the drive, the girls show me photos of the house on their phones. The place is huge, all glass. There's supposed to be a hot tub.

As Helena navigates the switch curls of the road, I eat two weed pills for no particular reason. At noon, halfway there, we stop at the coast for a hike. I don't really want to hike, but it's their vacation too, so I go. We clamber from the car and throw on sunglasses. I don't have any hiking gear or water, but it's sunny, cold wind off the water, a nice day. I'll survive.

The trail runs five kilometres next to the ocean. There are some muddy sections, but most of it's dry and rocky and passes through stands of cedar and arbutus, the trees bent away from the wind. We climb rock ledges to take pictures. Sprucing up our social media and future dating app profiles because you never know. The sun spins overhead like a siren, but the air is still frigid. I get so cold during chemo. I try not to shiver or let them see me shiver. Only wearing a sweater and old bomber jacket for this. My sister can tell I'm cold, I think, but we don't stop. After a couple hours, we're back at the car and ready to keep going.

Later, at the house, we drink beer and run barefoot across wet grass to the hot tub. Now that night's fallen, the cold is real. Freezing wind tears inland like sheet metal. I shouldn't drink beer when on the weed pills, or when in chemo in general, but I have one, then another, another. Maybe that's why I'm so cold. I shouldn't be doing this to my body, these substances on top of substances. Soon, even the hot tub isn't hot enough to keep me warm. I race inside and sit on the couch in my sweater and toque. I go to the panel on the wall and turn the heat up, then turn it up again. The tiles are so hot that I can feel them through my socks. Twenty minutes later, I've got all my sweaters on, and Helena's jacket, and I'm using pillows as tiny quilts around my body. I just need to sleep it off, I guess. Too much weed and beer.

I take a long shower with the hot water all the way up, which helps. Partway through shampooing, big clumps of my hair start to fall out. Hair washes into my eyes and mouth and starts to clog the drain. I've been holding off on cutting the hair for a few weeks, waited too long. With chemo, there's always a specific day when the hair goes. I try and scratch off as much hair as I can and stamp it down the drain. I'm in there long enough to feel bad about wasting water. After towelling off, I head to my room, saying goodnight, that it was fun, that we'll get brunch tomorrow.

For the next hour, I roll back and forth across the bed, shivering, able to feel my hair scattering across the pillow. When I do sleep, bad dreams come about shadow worlds where everything is made of a thick fabric. I'm so hot and can't tell if it's the dream or real. In the morning, I delay using the word *hospital* because no one likes that word. We get brunch. I feel the fever now. So obvious. How fevers sneak and bloom below other pain.

When they ask why I haven't eaten my brunch — crazily uncharacteristic of me — I do finally say the word *hospital*. We all get back in the car so they can take me to Jubilee back in Victoria, as that's the hospital I usually go to. At least being a cancer patient gets me admitted fast.

Again with the hospital. I check in and get moved quickly to a room on the main floor. I stay overnight with the infection. Another IV in my arm. Jell-O. Oatmeal. The thin blue quilts that I need five of. I can't get away, no matter how I try. The nurse is so nice taking care of me. I've seen her on the dating apps, for sure, but don't mention it. If she recognizes me, she also doesn't mention it.

I toss and turn all night again, too much light and noise, right next to the emergency department. I should get out tomorrow. A few more days still until the next treatment. Need to make them count, maybe go somewhere, maybe with friends, with family, do something fun.

•

I WAKE UNDER BLUE HOSPITAL bulbs. My eyes can't fully see yet, still half-anaesthetized, but I'm in bed. The bed is so warm and comfortable. A beeping sound cuts the silence. Mom is somewhere nearby, I think, can hear her nervous rustling. When I wake from surgeries, I always try to assess the things in my body that feel different, as if the missing bits of flesh will be specific and obvious. I try to feel the absent lymph node but am still so heavily drugged I can't focus. My eyes won't stay open, and I drift off again.

The beeping. Loud enough to wake me. Now, a voice at my side. "Okay, breathe in, and then out. There we go."

I breathe in and the beeping stops. Good. Back to sleep it is. The bed so warm. Floating there, unhurried.

The beeping.

"Okay, just another breath in now. That's good, and then another." The voice quiet, whispering.

Whenever I take a breath, the beeping stops, and whenever I don't, it resumes. All well and good. But breathing will take care of itself, as it always has. Better to sleep. The nurse — I see her now, next to the bed, purple scrubs, round-bodied — she won't let me sleep. She keeps asking me to breathe.

People move around the recovery room, opening drawers, wheeling beds to and fro. I can't focus my eyes, so I listen. Other nurses are talking about how it's not ideal that I still need someone to remind me to breathe. My penis hurts, maybe from the catheter. I say this aloud: "My penis hurts."

The nurse says, "Okay, that's fine, now just a little breath in, and then out, then another breath in. This machine will beep anytime you are not breathing."

Minutes tick past and my breathing stabilizes, and eventually, the nurse leaves and I'm left to my pain, which, now that I'm able to breathe again, is considerable. Whenever they cut through the abdominal wall to get at a tumour, no matter how small the modern-day robotic scissor arms, it hurts. At least my scars from these surgeries are small, most looking like freckles or moles. Laparoscopies involve one entry cut on each side of the abdomen, then a cut in through the belly button. One perforation gets a scissor arm, the other a camera, the third a tube to pump in nitrogen. They use nitrogen because inflated people are easier to operate on. The surgeon I saw during the consultation for this surgery was more worried than usual. Hemming and hawing about risk and danger. Seemed concerned about how close the lymph node they wanted was to my aorta. He emphasized that it's a blood vessel the circumference of a Red Bull can, which I didn't appreciate. That guy didn't end up doing the surgery. I got someone else.

You never really know what happens in a surgery. You go under, and you wake up, hopefully. If you do wake up, you get a result or outcome, but no one ever tells you what *went on*. I wonder if, at some point in any of these surgeries, I've died and been brought back. Or they've cut something they didn't mean to cut. Did they have to extend the surgery and give me more anaesthesia on the fly? That could be why the no breathing. Either way, when you sleep normally, you wake up knowing time has passed — there's a feel to it, a thickness. But with anaesthesia, you don't. There is no sense of time, just a great lunge through darkness, the body strapped down and taken apart on the thin hope that it's worth it, that this time will be different. And so far, it has always been worth it, but never been different.

•

REMISSION IS LIKE AIR: YOU only appreciate it when it's gone. After four years of not appreciating it, I'm back on Vancouver

Island, where I work at the university as a cafeteria dishwasher.
I'm back again at the place where I've been an undergrad, graduate
student, teaching assistant, instructor, and now dishwasher. They
truly cannot keep me away. So many jobs. This dishwashing gig is a
big step up after three years at the deli down the hill. I taught a few
classes during the deli era, it's true, but not enough to be full-time.
Sometimes, after running a writing workshop, I would walk down
for an evening of selling ham and wrestling racks of chickens from
the oven. If I spotted one of my students in the aisles, I'd hide in the
cooler so they wouldn't see me aproned and covered in meat juice.
How do you teach someone the sentence after that? You can't —
and sure as hell not character development or psychic distance. I
hid from them like you hide from anything that might dissolve an
already tenuous air of authority. Anyway, dishwashing pays almost
as much as sessional teaching did, which is a subject I'm not even
going to tackle here. If anyone asks what I do, I tell them I work in
an industrial kitchen — expediting, heavy machinery, catering. Say
this on dates. Never say *dishwasher*.

We work in a big wet coliseum behind the burger station, water
everywhere, grease aerosolized into tiny droplets that hang in the
air like foul rain. The floor is orange tile so slippery that we have a
long list of workplace injuries. Our main weapon is a twenty-foot
conveyor washer that needs to clean dishes for the eighteen hundred
students living on campus. We wield pressure washers, steel wool,
long brushes, and special kinds of bleach. Different foods require
different tools to remove. Can't send baked-on cheese through the
machine. Never. Soften it first with hours in the vat. Lasagna day,
macaroni day — they're long.

One person loads the conveyor, and one unloads it. There's a
rhythm, a flow, a way to rack dishes onto the conveyor's tines so

that it is always moving. Watch the guys who've been here ten years, fifteen years; they know. Each has his own way. I load plates every second tine because it's fast but gives the person unloading enough leeway to keep up. Sometimes, when my friend Sergio is on un- loading duty, I load plates every seventh tine as a joke. When he notices, he looks around his end of the machine at me and rolls his eyes. He's Chilean. He and I talk politics, radicalization, the evils of capitalism. He's a good friend.

I start reading too many abstracts again, every day worried about the cancer coming back.

My work shirts get so stained with grease that I throw them in the garbage and steal more from the supply closet. Black goo builds up in the soles of my shoes, a gel of crushed food and the congealed fat that spills off meat trays, until the shoes start to smell bad. Sometimes, when I'm working alone, I pressure-wash the soles in the big sink, the goo coming off like spiral macaroni. Disgusting. I bleach the sink afterward. When I'm not wearing them, the shoes stay in the changing room with all the other black shoes stacked in lockers and shoved into nooks. People just know which ones are theirs.

In the spring of that first year of dishwashing, I have some back pain. Not from the labour, though. I play it off as a kidney stone, but I know what pain like this means. My doctors do an MRI. It's not a kidney stone, of course. It's never a kidney stone. And after the diagnosis comes down, that kidney pain disappears for- ever, which leaves me wondering where it came from in the first place.

I don't tell my managers about the cancer coming back yet. Not the right time. Only when the chemotherapy's looming will telling them make sense — being sad isn't a good enough excuse. I keep

going to work but take longer breaks, maybe too long, sometimes
way too long. I also start to use too many of the blue nitrile gloves
we're offered — so many, hundreds, like I'm trying to kill the rainforest single-handedly. But something about the diagnosis has me
unwilling to get even the smallest bit of leftover food on my skin.
The old me used to switch gloves only when they tore, but now it's
a new pair after a bit of oil, a smudge of peanut butter, some stray
Cheerios. With gloves on, I don't feel texture, only temperature.
It seems like the others pick up on my new glove mania and also
start using more, just shredding the supply. A few hard-core types
never wear them. Older guys, mostly. One in particular, who has
been here more than forty years, works bare-handed in the sludge
students leave behind: ketchup poured into soda, sweet and sour
sauce mixed into milk.

Each tray of refuse gets hand-sorted into the correct recycling
and compost bins. Students leave gum on their trays, maybe not
understanding that if we miss it, it melts in the machine, hair-thin
strands covering everything like spiderwebs. A nightmare to clean.
And don't get me started on coffee grounds: entire loads speckled
black and needing to be sent through again. If one of us sends coffee
grounds through, we hear about it.

It's hard working full-time with the cancer, though mercifully
most of the kitchen staff get laid off in the summer and go on
employment insurance. And then off to Japan for my cousin's wedding, after which my imagination sees only a void I try not to consider. What will the doctors do next? I can't get another transplant
of my own stem cells; that's a one-off. Someone else's? I can check
with my siblings, I guess. The odds are one in four — not bad.
Or maybe some new chemo, gene therapy. There are all kinds of
experimental treatments in the pipeline, though patients in trials
sometimes die from cytokine storms, like human-shaped infernos. I
use all my sick days, then my vacation days, then take leave without

pay here and there until they say I can't do that anymore if I want to keep working here.

The dishwashing crew is a mix of immigrant students, lifers, and younger locals just happy to no longer be working at grocery stores. The immigrants are mostly smart guys from Egypt and India doing part-time shifts while they get their Ph.D.s in electrical engineering, chemistry, computer science. The lifers are mostly white smokers, waiting on their pensions. The younger locals are like me: wayward, happy to manage rent with a bit left over. One morning in September, recently back from the summer break, it's me and a guy from Nigeria. He has a law degree and is finishing an MBA. Nice guy, always rapping under his breath and talking about girls. The dining room is closed for an event and all the cafeteria tables are stacked up, so there's not much to do. The boss tells us to chisel the gum from the undersides of the tables. He gives us butter knives from the cutlery shelf to use. For a minute or two we stand there, not wanting to chisel gum, but then we get going. The older gum pops right off. Fresh gum takes time. There's a lot of it. Pink. Grey. Green. Gum pulled into strings. Gum balled up like tiny planets. We devise a system: flip each table together, work from either end toward the middle, then restack it off to the side. Once all the tables have been chiselled, the boss tells us to put them back in place for the next day.

I'm a few weeks past the abdominal surgery to find out what kind of cancer it is. I still haven't told my managers. I'll tell them soon, will have to tell them soon. Once the doctors put that node under a microscope, things will be clearer. Is it the same cancer as before, or something new? Hopefully the same. New is bad with these things. In my case, new would be large diffuse B-cell lymphoma — a mutation you don't want, very bad news. Your odds of mutation increase with your number of years in the game. How many has it been now? Ten? Eleven? My percentages are climbing.

At least the incisions from past surgeries healed well, though there's a divot below my belly button I suspect will be there forever. Definite swelling in my legs, too, but I can't do anything about that. Damage to the lymphatic system does not heal.

Some of the young catering guys help us set up the tables. We work fast, like it's a competition. Table legs shriek against the wood floor. Joints lock into place. Chair towers are wheeled from storage and spread throughout the room, guys plucking chairs off the top and slamming them into rows.

I'm flipping a table near a big potted fern when something tears in my abdomen. A shearing. Internal. I know that if it hurts now, it'll hurt more later, after the muscles cool down, but there are only a few tables left. I keep going: flip a table, centre it, flip another. The tables are red and shiny, and soon the pain dulls until I don't even think about it, focused only on the table in front of me, and the next, and the next, each one nudged into place with a steel rattle.

The dining room's big windows cheer me up. Bright sun. Sky so blue. Our last drip of summer. Big hemlocks sway on the lawn surrounded by old concrete residence buildings. I'm not sure what's happening inside me, but I'm almost done for the day, almost out the door. It'll all come clear soon. Each time is easier; each time is harder. Get through it. Rebuild like everyone else does. My rebuilding is different each time, but also the same: Hospital stays. Needle bruises. Blood dripping off my elbow. Nights on the edge of my bed in the darkness. The nausea saying *Go*, saying *Transform*. And you do transform, though not right then. Only later. Only when you're not ready.

•

FOR THREE DAYS, THE POST-SURGICAL mystery in my abdomen stays at a low simmer. I rationalize. After all, The Body heals in its own way. I already have cancer — what more is there? Then Monday comes, and I wake up *sore*. The soreness deep inside, left groin, emanating. I don't have any sick days left, so I go in to wash dishes like every other day. We get through the breakfast rush in a few hours, eggs always the worst of it, plates needing hours in the bleach tank and I still have to scrape them with a tool more typically used to spread paint. Around 11:00 a.m. the pain worsens. Feverish now. Trembling. I hide in the bathroom for long stretches. I go to the cafeteria manager, say I've had a surgery, don't say what for. Say I might have done something while flipping the tables on Friday, maybe ruptured internal sutures. He gets me to fill out insurance paperwork in case of compensation claims down the line. My shirt is stuck to me, and I lean against the office door and nod and say everything will be fine.

At home I take a leftover tramadol prescribed after a previous surgery. I will avoid the hospital. I don't like it there, don't like being there, living there.

All day I'm in bed, taking various pills from the bathroom. Tylenol. More tramadol. The opiate feels good and throws a layer of fuzz at the corner of my eye. By evening, the fever abates.

Next morning, I wake up wreathed in agony. Tremors run down my arms so violently I can't handle my phone. I hyperventilate. All limbs curl into a spiderlike ball. For some minutes, I follow the breath and meditate. This is only pain. Pain is temporary. It's my reaction to the pain that is truly painful. Right? Right! The second arrow! Just like the Buddha said. When I'm settled enough, I call home, and Mom picks up. I begin asking for her nurse opinion, but can't finish before I burst into tears, it hurts so much. She's panicking on the other end. I shouldn't have done this to her; I haven't cried in ten years. I crawl to the bathroom for more tramadol and a digital thermometer. Once back in bed, I grip the phone between my ear and sweat-damp shoulder. She tries to comfort me but says I should go to the hospital. My duvet is drenched. Soon, the thermometer beeps and a red screen pops up showing 103 degrees Fahrenheit. I didn't know the screen could turn red. The pain is so bad I can't extend my abdomen to stand straight and have to walk bent almost double. Does cancer do this? I can't tell anymore.

Not wanting to freak any of my friends out, I call an ambulance and pack an overnight bag and toothbrush and my laptop and the chargers and cords I'll need if they keep me there.

I meet the paramedics in the apartment building lobby, limping, my left leg/abdomen/groin area not functioning at all. I tell them some of my medical history, the recent surgery, all that, and they get me to sit on a stretcher in the back of the ambulance. As the vehicle pulls away from the curb, my phone falls onto the corrugated metal floor. The screen breaks.

They admit me into the emergency room, take my temperature, the regular stuff. Still feverish, I try and explain the pain without sounding like a drug seeker, but they don't give me anything. I'm led to the waiting room. People in casts or clutching red-stained bandages to extremities. One guy rants about Germans and Augustus Caesar and how they fought for control of a crucial bridge. A huge security guard lumbers over and tells the ranting guy it's his last warning about Augustus Caesar. There's a placard near the intake desk that shows the average wait time is three hours. I hunker down. Eventually, the tramadol wears off. I huff and puff in my chair, each sound half groan, half breath. I cannot stop making the pain sounds and people are getting uncomfortable. Hours tick by.

When a doctor finally sees me, he asks all kinds of questions, feels my testicles, my groin, everywhere. Doesn't think it's anything, somehow. They take blood from both arms for a bacterial culture. After confirming my pain level, they inject me with hydro-morphone. When I ask for ondansetron to pair with the painkiller because of past experiences with opiate nausea, the nurse shoots me a look like *Aren't you a pharmaceutical connoisseur!* But she still gives it to me. I'm sent back to the waiting room. Two more hours crawl by, but easier now, opiate high, cradled in its warm depth. When the doctor calls me in again, he's spoken with the surgeon who did my abdominal procedure those weeks back to cut out a lymph node. The surgeon told him nothing could be wrong with me, he doesn't think it's anything, to just take Tylenol and keep my fever under control and go home.

•

I GO HOME, WHERE I take much-increased doses of Tylenol, and the fever dips further. Pain persists, though, as does the sweating. Yet they sent me home at the behest of the surgeon, so it must be fine. For four days I languish in bed, fever up and down with the intake of Tylenol. The nights are bad. Sweating so much I need to flip my blanket and sleep on a towel, also flipping the towel, getting another towel. By Tuesday it's so bad I get in the shower at 3:00 a.m., and I'm sweating so bad the water can't touch my skin. The sweat feeling like a fish's mucus layer. I book in to see my oncologist. He meets me at the cancer centre. I am all fucked up. I ask him what is going on. He, too, spoke with the surgeon. He expresses some concern that I could have an infection but mentions that the surgeon told him not to worry, it's all good, it's fine. I'm sent home again.

On Friday I call the surgeon personally and ask to meet. He keeps a walk-in clinic a forty-minute bus ride from my apartment and tells me to arrive at seven in the morning if I want to be seen. I bus there the next day in soft, yellow dawn light, shivering, so weak I'm leaning against lampposts in the clinic parking lot. It's sunny and cold, and I wait outside the locked doors until a secretary opens the place up. Once inside, I take a number, like all the other haggard people in line. And then it's my turn. The surgeon is tall, buzz cut, handsome. He's unconcerned. Gives me a quick checkup. Says it might be a spot of infection, but definitely *not* as a result of his surgery. That would be impossible. He writes me a scrip for amoxicillin and sends me away.

I take the amoxicillin through Sunday but don't get better. Sick enough now that it feels like a chemotherapy, but one that gets worse every day instead of better. This whole fucking thing is like more chemo, super-powered chemo, killing me. Sunday night I return to the hospital, like *Please let me in.* The nice folks in emergency are perplexed at my return. Aren't I fine? Wasn't I dealt with? More blood tests are ordered. This time they throw in a CT scan of my left abdomen.

There's a second waiting room off the side of the main waiting room. This room has chairs that recline and IV stands and a blanket warmer. I'm given a spot in this room and sit there all night, in and out of sleep, feverish, again changing clothes around 3:00 a.m. because of the sweat.

At some point in the morning, they get the CT results back. I'm escorted beyond the doors of the second waiting room into the hospital proper and given a new, curtained room. A doctor sees me immediately, concern in her eyes, says I'm extremely sick. Alarmingly sick. Thank God I came when I did. They need to admit me now. There's an abscess the size of an apple in my lower left abdomen. Of course. Why not? The infection in my blood. Septic. An infectious disease specialist comes in next, wondering what I've been doing at home, why I'm not hospitalized. She says this is serious. Do I understand how serious this is? Do I? They start antibiotics, the big stuff, nuclear level. The blood cultures last week must've shown nothing, but now they take more samples, more needles, my elbows leaking little red drops into the taped-on cotton balls. The cultures take forty-eight hours, so they don't know yet what it is, and I'll have to sit tight.

As I recline in the bed, shivering, three different student doctors come for my medical history, one after another, two women, one man, all young and tired looking, the guy in expensive dress clothes, the women in scrubs. I have an almost eidetic memory when it comes to my medical history and can rattle off chemo after chemo, exact surgeries, drug lists, duration, cycle length, prognosis, dates, times. I wish I remembered the good things, the joy, the forests. Over the next hour, I tell each student doctor a slightly different medical history. Changing the tone of my voice, the pacing, the emphasis on different events. Because it's funny. Because I'm upset. Could be it's a contest and one of them gets fired if they don't diagnose me correctly. Could be just an opportunity for residents to get a look at someone whose suffering is interesting. There's the sense my infection is life threatening and *very* serious. They keep saying the word *serious* and look aghast and embarrassed after I tell them the complete narrative arc of my attempts to be hospitalized. This must all be very expensive.

The hospital's overrun. I wait another fifteen hours or so in the makeshift room until they move me to the fourth floor. This room is already full, two men in it. The orderlies craft a nook for me in the corner, with a rolling fabric divider on one side for privacy. The roommate by the window is about fifty, reading a book, all kinds of tubes going into him, beige slurry in the tubes — he might not have a stomach. The other roommate is old, asleep or unconscious, his blankets flipped back to show most of his pelvis, his atrophied legs, liver spots like camouflage. A catheter tube runs from the tangle of blankets off the side of his bed to a half-filled bag of orange liquid. It's indecent, but that's what sickness is; that's what dying is.

They continue with the antibiotics, trying this and that. I'm not getting better. Still can't really walk. The infectious disease doctor is a tall, olive-skinned woman with curly hair, and she visits several times that night to tell me how sick I am and that they are doing everything they can. The abscess is still there, festering. I text updates to my family. My sister Angela is flying down from Yukon. I miss her. I text the manager of the cafeteria a picture of my IV stand and admission wristband, so he knows I won't be washing dishes in the near term. It would be nice if Mom came down, but I don't think she can see me like this anymore. Too many times like this. Too many emergencies. I get it.

•

IN ONE CORNER OF THE ward there's a small, many-windowed room with two beige couches. I sit with my laptop and close my eyes every few minutes to stare at the sun. There hasn't been sun for days, and its red glow burns through my eyelids. A bag of pus swings back and forth from where it exits my hip; a pink safety clip keeps it attached to my shirt so the tube doesn't pull. I try not to touch the tube itself, the itch of it, the perforation. I only want out of here. Here again, always here.

Down the hall sits an old lady in a wheelchair. She's far off but moving. Toward me. I can't see with all the sun. I go back to the laptop and other people's pictures of meadows and puppies and snow-dappled mountains. Soon, I notice the old lady closer still. She's dragging herself forward an inch at a time with her right foot. Reach, drag, reach, drag. Little steps. Staring at me. I put the laptop down and wait, certain I'm her destination. It takes some time. Her body in the blue hospital gown is a scaffold. Long grey hair in all directions. Head canted to one side. Dragging the wheelchair inch by inch. And eventually, she arrives at the small room and drags herself the five feet to where I sit. Now very close. Mint smell. Frayed veins in her cheeks. With a jerk, she swings out and grabs my wrist, holds tight. I almost fall over. She looks in my eyes and doesn't say a word. Then a nurse sees and comes over and gets her to let me go, guides the chair away, saying she should have a snack, a bath, that there is so much to do.

•

AS DAD AND I LEAVE the cancer centre, I pull a small chocolate weed brownie out of my pack and eat it in three quick bites. The rain smells like dust. My cousin Peter has been making the brownies for me — dark chocolate, just sweet enough, almost burnt. He'll make a big batch, take half for his roommates and himself, and give me the rest. I should thank him more, or do something nice for him, when I'm better. I took the Emend earlier, one hour before the treatment like they tell me to. Always being careful with that pill, since they're fifty dollars. Or at least that's what I pay — no idea what the actual cost is, maybe hundreds. Emend is a two-pack meant to be used the day of chemo and the day after, and I don't want to imagine what the nausea would be like without it. On the R-CHOP now. The big bad R-CHOP chemo. I'd *heard* about R-CHOP in my general reading about cancer, and, yes, was like, *Jesus Christ, it's called CHOP?* But I never expected to be on it personally. It is quite something.

We get in the waiting cab and head to my apartment. Dad asking if I need soup, saying that I should have soup, that soup is good for me. The ride isn't long. We hop out on Yates Street in the shadow of a big hemlock. I walk slow. He comes up to the apartment to make sure I'm okay, though it's a space maybe too small for two people. He likes to stay with me after chemotherapy, almost like he thinks that's the most awful time. The worst time is still to come, usually day three or four, but I don't say that. He reclines onto the old flower-print chesterfield Joan MacLeod gave me years ago. She was my playwriting professor in first year, one of the best. I haven't seen her in a while, but her old couch persists.

The first hours blur to a paste. Dad falls asleep on the couch at a crazy angle, his snores loud and random. Pins and needles hit my feet. My eyes swell. The heat of these drugs. Like being stuffed face-first into a sleeping bag. So much going on in my body that I just sit there, stoned out of my mind, and play the most tedious video games. There's this one where you have a kingdom and need to explore and wage war with magical heroes, all turn-based, with little movement tiles, everything needing to be so precise, kind of like chess mixed with *The Lord of The Rings*. This is a good chemo game: it's time consuming, engrossing, there's no rush or mechanical skill required, and, most important, you don't have to play against a real person. I can only handle playing against the computer right now. Even a digital interaction with someone else would be too much.

All day I hit the vaporizer and eat brownies. I can't fucking believe I'm using marijuana again, after it so destroyed my life those years back. But here we are. Situations change. The nausea is bad enough that weed has somehow become medicine. And it helps me eat. Eventually, Dad snuffles awake and asks what time it is and if I need anything, maybe soup. I say no, that I'm just doing nothing, that he can go back to his hotel. We hug. He says to call if anything comes up.

I game for four or five more hours, until I have a hard time focusing my eyes. Sleep isn't the great getaway you might think while on chemo, so I stay up late. Sleep is particularly vulnerable, as that's when the nausea creeps up. You want to always stay ahead of nausea. Nausea is like love — once it's next to you, it's beyond you. Then you are chasing it and hopeless. But I curl up on top of my quilt all the same, and shiver and sweat and imagine a world where I can fly, and all the issues I'd have flying, like hitting electrical wires or birds or whether I would only do it at night so the government wouldn't imprison me and conduct tests. Like this, I fall asleep. A few hours later, I wake dizzy and sick to my stomach, the nausea having crept.

I'm curled into a ball much too tight for how inflexible I am. If you let your guard down for a fucking second or feel unsick for a few minutes and get it in your head that maybe you can skip a dose of ondansetron, nausea will come after you with everything. There's a limit to how much ondansetron I can take each day, and it's so expensive, so I roll from bed and root through the bathroom drawer for the prochlorperazine, which I always hope not to need. Prochlorperazine was a first-gen antipsychotic, but it's prescribed for nausea as well. And it *does* work, though it sometimes flattens me into one dimension.

I sit there as the vaporizer warms on my bedside table, it's yellow light that denotes *not hot enough* like a tiny nebula in the darkness. I've already filled it with Super Silver Haze, the only strain of weed that doesn't give me anxiety attacks, doesn't make me afraid, and lets me eat food. I swallow the prochlorperazine with some lemon water and sit on the bed, puffing the vaporizer. Even when the vape is empty, I still puff on it, the warm air tickling my throat. I delay sleep, not wanting to close my eyes. Closed eyes are dangerous. I pick at my cuticles. I stare at the wall. The lamp casts rigid shadows on the white paint and I notice an old handprint above the bed. I think it's mine. I remember her — a good memory. But I should still clean more and notice stuff like this.

A few hours later, I wake again, thirsty and burning up. It's not a fever, but that's how it feels. The R-CHOP in full swing now, bursting cells. The war in me at a crescendo. As cancer cells die during chemo, they enter the bloodstream as a great river of trash. I pace to the kitchen and drink a litre of water. What a foul taste. With chemo, mouth cells die off first and form a zombie paste at the back of your tongue.

I lie back down and put an Ativan under my tongue — though you're not really supposed to mix benzos with weed — and drift off. The nausea will be back by morning, and we'll begin again. This goes on for ten days. Right around the time I'm too exhausted to notice or struggle anymore, the nausea will fade. I'll sit there in the blank afternoon light from the window, grateful, wondering what I'm meant to do. And ten days after that is the next infusion, and so it will be for the next five months. They get worse as you go, the treatments. As the drugs build up in the body, as your strength goes. By next cycle, I'll feel the tumours being attacked, how they flare once the cells start to die en masse. All through my abdomen I'll feel this reactive heat in specific areas that I think match the tumour locations mentioned in the CT scan report. I don't know if this is real, but I feel it. Part of me loves to feel the cancer die even as parts of me die with it. The feeling of the cancer reacting always goes away by month four, or it has so far, though one day in the future it probably won't go away, or won't begin at all, and that's what I think about.

•

DURING THE R-CHOP, I START to cry for about five minutes before going to sleep each night. The first few times, I'm like, *Oh God, what is going on? This must be a side effect of the drugs.* Obviously. The crying helps me sleep more than anything else, more than weed, more than Ativan. I don't remember the last time I cried. I'm so sick, my insides boiling. I'll be in bed, in the dark, listening to my fridge, and it's like I can finally *allow* the tears to come. I try not to be too loud, don't want the guy who lives above to hear. You can do it in the shower, if you have to. Water is good cover. Maybe it just builds up. So many years of this. Of sitting in the dark with drugs burning a hole through me. Bulbous with steroids, curled over, every cell wracked. R-CHOP is worse than the others. I'm getting older and slower to heal, slower to metabolize. Five months of injections strain me. During the days, I eat weed, I languish, I game. I do squats in the hallway, or dumbbell curls, or go outside for walks with the sun hitting me like a stove element. Relapsed on weed, after all my work. Funny world. I don't even like getting high anymore, no joy when I do it, whatever void it used to fill no longer there, and maybe that's progress and the therapy I've been doing.

By day eleven of each cycle, I stop the weed and don't start again until the next one, no temptation whatsoever, and that feels good, like I've healed at least one part of me. I always think about how Gabor Maté said that not all traumatized people are addicts, but that every addict is a traumatized person. God damn. And then I'll go outside wearing three sweaters, walking through rain and wind, not to anywhere in particular, just in circles, around the block, around two blocks.

By the twelfth day, I can see Ronnie. She'll come over, radiant, carrying a glass container of bright-red kimchi stew that we eat together. I miss her during the first eleven days of each cycle but don't ask her to come over and don't try to visit her. There's something wrong with my doing that, I know. I haven't told her I love her yet, though I should, I know I should. What with how it might all turn out, what with disease. I'll get around to it. There will be a better time. I don't want to be the one saying *I love you* while maybe dying. Don't want it to be from the movies, where I say I love her, and then right before I die, we get married and it's, like, *so* sad and everyone remembers it forever. I will not have that. I just want it to be a regular *I love you*, unburdened by conditions or reality. And that's probably the wrong goal, but I've held off saying it and will keep holding off. All I know is it's good to have someone during this, different than the other times.

•

I'M IN A HOSPITAL ROOM, or some kind of hospice, bedridden. The room's light is white and blue. I want the light to be yellow, but it's not yellow. I'm maybe thirty-three years old, thirty-four. Probably single. Wasted away. My skin is grey. I'm all bones and gauntness. On painkillers now, lots of them, home stretch. Hardly aware what is happening, asleep most of each day. No, actually I am aware, fully aware. I can see molecules, can see time. My family has come; they pass in and out of the room, trying to smile. Their all being there makes me realize it'll be soon. Bleach smell. Body odour. Vinegar. The bed is uncomfortable and cuts into my back. I hear Mom crying, but in the hallway, if there's a hallway. My siblings sit there when they think I'm asleep, often looking at their phone, waiting for it. They all have lives to live, probably children — they will go on without me, the way humans do. It's too hot; it's too cold. I'm thinking about playing in the sand as a kid, a fishhook in my palm. I'm angry. Why don't I get a chance? So much wasted time. Now this big financial burden on my retiring parents. I'm not on chemo anymore. We're beyond that. The taste in my mouth is of old meat, the salivary glands raw and exposed. I can't eat, though I'm hungry. Morning light through the window. I want the window opened but don't say so. I don't know what day it is. I regret not getting married, not having children. Sick forever, how could I? Soon to be alone. I can't move much. I cry. I don't want to leave my family behind. My niece, my siblings, my mom and dad. They are so dear to me, and now I must go on without them.

•

I'M WAITING AGAIN IN ONE of the cancer centre's orange rooms. A nurse has weighed me — the number high, will need to be diligent — and I've been told to sit until the oncologist comes in. I cross my legs and drape an arm over the chair back as if not extremely concerned. *This* meeting is always done at the end of chemo and after the PET scan to discuss moving forward if I'm once again cancer-free — which I am. The scan came back negative. Each time the feeling is different, this being negative. Where does the cancer go? Wherever it goes can't be that great, because it always comes back right as my life begins to stabilize. But no. That's magical thinking. The truth is I have some genetic flaw, an error in my code. I know this. And though the cancer is gone, that code remains, *I* remain, and the process will repeat. Cells growing out of control, my immune system incapable of noticing or coping with the invasive growth.

Hurried footsteps sound in the hallway. The doctor walks in with a big smile. We shake hands. He asks how I'm doing, says it's good to see me, that I look good. He stands next to the sink, washing his hands, making more small talk. How do I feel? What is going on in my life? Not much, doc. Not much. Reassembling. He's a nice guy, really. Good at his job.

I hop onto the examination table before he asks me to. He does the usual checks: my neck, my armpits, has me lie down and raps his knuckles up and down my torso, perhaps seeking weird echo noises among my organs — I don't remember why they do this. And then he listens to my lungs: breathe in, breathe out, good, good.

Almost six months of chemo and now this. I'm tired. To be done again overwhelms. Every few years having to get through. He wants me to be happy about the negative scan, I think, to rejoice and celebrate. But I'm not, and I don't. After so much danger, I am now always with the danger, is the sense. I don't like being this way. But all the therapy and meditation and self-care just can't undo what's happened. Good news and bad news often feel the same. You get so used to fighting and then can't turn it off. He says I'm looking fit, and it's all very promising.

"So," he says, serious again. "I don't think we can say this will last."

The hurt comes.

"Yeah," I say. "Guess that's unlikely."

"We need to be realistic," he says, hands tightly squeezed. "Lots of good treatments coming out, but if you relapsed this time and relapsed the previous time, we need to assume it will come back at some point."

I nod too much, amiable. I will agree and be realistic. I will turn toward the truth like the therapist said, will accept reality on reality's terms.

"But hopefully I don't see you for ten years," he goes on. "Hopefully, this is a durable remission."

Durable. This isn't the first time he's used the word. Boy, do I miss the days of them saying *cured.* Those were the good, unrealistic times. Am I to be *durable* now? Cancer will be splashed across me like juice onto tile, only to be wiped away, then again splashed and again wiped away.

We say our goodbyes. He's busy. Many patients in the pipeline, most of them probably not getting such good news. I try to be mindful that most patients don't get to be so familiar with these orange hallways, don't get to fear them, don't get to feel like they live here. But that's not true either. One visit is fear. One visit is a lifetime. I walk past the bakery counter and out the glass doors, hoping I can stay away for ten years, hoping I don't recognize a single nurse when I return, that there's a whole new roster waiting for me. Ten years would be nice. Could build so much in ten years. Maybe they'll have repainted by then, no more orange, now blue, now white. I need only be more durable than paint.

As I pass into the summer sun, I realize I should have asked about the ten years. Should have got it in writing. Ten years. Guaranteed. What will be happening in ten years? What can I get done by then? For sure I'll need a stable job, a job I can leave and then return to after, if there is an after. Ten fucking years. A wife? Children? If I still can, if the frozen samples work out, if I have fifty thousand dollars to make that work. Ten years. My little kid wondering what's wrong with me. Why can't Dad play? Why can't Dad get out of bed?

Can I do that to someone? Who would dare? Ten years. For sure keep running. Eat the garlic and spinach. Vitamins. Lifting weights. Cardio. Ten years is something. More than most. I should be so lucky. People die all the time out of nowhere. This is what the professionals tell me. People die — they don't expect it, but still die. Pianos fall on people. People are hit by cartoon mallets and become pancake representations of themselves. This happens *all the time.* My knowing what comes for me is no different, is it? Cancer is the piano is the mallet. You get in the car and you are dead. Something in your brain lets go and you are dead. Cancer should not bother me, not anymore; it is one of many things that chase and come for us, and my knowing its face and its name does not make it more dangerous. I tell myself this. Every day I say it and say it and write in my journal that I am not in any particular danger. But still I wish I did not know, and that it could all go on and on and I'd never realize or think about it or understand.

•

I'M DRIVING JULI AROUND SALTILLO in Uncle Pedro's Kia. We haven't explored much yet, but she's had her eye on the Catedral de Santiago, the towering white stone church at the centre of town. Together only eight months, but here I am. I've never driven in Mexico before and the rules seem different. No signalling for lane changes or turning. Speed bumps everywhere. Tons of little trucks with rakes and hoses and ladders in the back. My dad would love these trucks to carry small amounts of things. Can't buy little trucks in Canada anymore, impossible. She navigates for me, or I would get lost, and sometimes she says the wrong thing and we do get lost, and she apologizes, and I apologize for making her feel it necessary to apologize, and we have our Canadian moment, then kiss and keep going.

Once downtown, we drive through a warren of dusky, wall-girded streets. I find a small pay parking lot next to the cathedral's grounds. Hand in hand, we stroll to Saltillo's central square. All the streets and stones and buildings are a tan colour. The desert air is hot and smells blue. Water gushes from a fountain covered in polit-ical signs I can't understand, and the feeling of being in the square is otherworldly — not because I'm in a different country, but more because love has me feeling outside of myself. Pigeons swarm and march in rows across the paving stones. A man plays a piano and sings in the shade of a black umbrella. What a deep voice. I hear "*Lo siento, lo siento*" and guess it must be very tragic.

The cathedral is closed, which is too bad, as it's quite magnifi-cent and huge and I think Juli really wanted to show me the inside. She's Catholic, obviously, and I'm not, but I can appreciate archi-tecture and history.

We instead go across the street to a museum focused on the his-tory of Saltillo. After sanitizing our shoes on an alcohol-soaked rug, we tiptoe through a maze of little hallways lined with remnants of old buildings, paintings, and various Jesuses on various crucifixes.

Jesus shown as skeletal, as muscular, as clean, as drenched in blood, one after the other. Then we enter a preserved bank vault and exhibits with chunks of stone and tools and paper documents covered in tiny handwritten Spanish, their edges curled and looking delicate as sunburned skin.

She translates as we go. This is an old city. They are all old cities here, centuries old, the first conquistadores coming in the 1500s to exterminate the Indigenous peoples.

We go to an art gallery in an old, repurposed manor house. Every floorboard creaks like a felled tree. The place all dark wood and shadow and switchback staircases. Each room displays the work of a different artist. Oil painting. Photography. One entire display with photos of Indigenous people in clown outfits, standing out in the desert among mangled yucca or in the rubble of what look like abandoned villages or partially built highways. I can't tell if it's some cultural sphere or artistic statement or both, and I don't think Juli knows either. She's been away for a long time.

Soon, we walk back to the park with the pigeons and sit on a bench in the sun. There's a breeze now, the air swept one way then another, the pigeons more organized than before. The man is still playing his piano and singing. I rest with my eyes closed. She's next to me, my arm around her warmth. I'm thinking about how she suggested I come to Mexico for the various lymphatic surgeries I've been looking into. Her uncle is a surgeon and has connections. It would be cheaper, if it ended up helping. No more cyclic infections. Maybe. But I resist this level of intervention. Part of me doesn't want her family pulled into the gravity of cancer, even if it's inevitable with how much I care for her.

Across the street there's a restaurant, the tables in a vine-covered courtyard. I'm hungry, even if my stomach hasn't been doing so well this week and I've been spending lots of time in the bathroom. I get a beer. She gets an orange juice. A pigeon waddles around our feet. For some reason, after looking at the menu, I order a burger, even though I don't want one. She orders enchiladas. And when the burger arrives it's huge and sloppy and not that bad, but I can't finish it. I nurse a second beer, and we talk about the drive back, where we'll stop, whether we need anything at the pharmacy off the highway.

Dusk has settled over the city by the time we return to the parking lot. Orange light fans the street, giving a sharp edge to each noble shadow. We fumble for some pesos and pay the attendant. The streets are tiny, and I get lost again. We are downtown now, on the main street, looking for a pharmacy. Trucks and vans scoot by and weave together in the unmarked lanes. I'm just trying not to bang up her uncle's car, driving slow, still signalling like an idiot. We eventually find the right street and head north, back to Arteaga, passing police trucks with two men strapped into the box with machine guns. It must be uncomfortable, having to stand like that all day in summer, with the helmets, the flak jackets. So much of what I've seen of Mexico is from films: the violence, the killings, all for the escape-giving drugs that pass through here. Some things are the same: the rainbow hillsides of shacks and houses in the shadow of red mountains. The air so clear. And some things are different. Like the tiny river running through Arteaga, a landmark I don't understand. The flow is only a foot wide and runs through the centre of town under giant, gnarled trees with names carved in their wood and families gathered around the carvings to take pictures. The river is quite clean, revered even, based on how the children play, leaping over it like their parents have told them to behave in its presence. But I still don't understand. Is it the only water? I haven't seen much water, it's true, and when I asked her uncle why everything uses gas for power, he just said, "Electricity is very expensive," which made sense when I thought about it.

•

DAD MEETS ME OUTSIDE THE centre's sliding glass doors. He's wearing torn hiking gear, patches at the knees, all fleece and Gore-Tex. The sky is a grey mass. I wonder how his feet are doing with all the walking on concrete. He walks everywhere on these cancer visits, so used to the Yukon wilderness that he forgets there are other ways to travel. Always walking five or six kilometres from his hotel to the clinic. He'll get a slight limp partway through the trip.

The cancer centre is right beside Victoria's Royal Jubilee Hospital, which is nice, as when you are obliterated it helps that they're close together. The hospital buildings are a dark tangerine, several of them new or under construction; the cancer centre is a pale tan but only three stories tall, with more windows and plants and deceptions of comfort.

We sanitize our hands at the pump station next to the door. Dad looks like he's had several cups of coffee, and the only clue to his worry is the hooklike shape of his fingers. I walk ahead, he follows, and we make our way to the appointment desk for the chemotherapy clinic. At the desk, I sanitize my hands again, the clear alcohol goo stinging in the cracks along my cuticles.

The receptionist looks up. How can they help me? Am I here for an appointment? Yes. Oh good, big smile, what's your name? She scrolls through a calendar on her computer monitor, sees my name, nods to herself. I know what comes next. With a closer inspection of my face, she asks if I feel capable of doing the infusion today. They always ask. *Are you able to do chemo today?* Are you? You're supposed to lie and say yes. I learned this interaction years ago, but still brace myself for it. She sits there waiting for the answer. So I say the lie, say yes, I am capable, am ready. She nods and makes a note in the computer. People must say no sometimes, right? Otherwise, why tempt me? The question makes it seem possible to avoid what is about to happen, to just walk out and be done.

Dad and I take seats in the small row of padded beige chairs. It's good to have him here, though there's a particular anguished vibe when he sits through these treatments. I get the sense he doesn't ever want to be in hospitals. His own father died from a brain tumour when my dad was sixteen. How this must be for him, doing it again and again. The family has been coming through the past months, as in other times. Previous cycles, it's been someone else: Mom, Alex, Jess, Angela. Rare times, nobody comes down and I go alone, and that's hard. But I get it. People have lives. I'm an adult now. Adults endure alone. I take an Ativan while waiting on the beige chair, then another. Benzos dull the edge and make me unaware of what's happening, for now.

A nurse in blue scrubs approaches and asks that we follow her. She leads us down the hall to the treatment room. So many years in this same room — the days blend together. There's me as a young man in college, cheeks all rosy; then older me, leaner, more afraid, thinking I will die; and now older again, maybe too old, overthinking. Floor-to-ceiling windows look onto hedgerows and a helicopter pad, and beyond that a school's green soccer field. The chemo chairs are arranged in a sloppy circle, one ring of chairs facing in, a few in the centre facing out. I always hope for a corner chair. Corner chairs let me face the rest of the room and keep an eye on things. But this time they're all occupied, all filled with old people. The nurse instead seats me in one of the middle island chairs, the centre of attention, everyone able to see what happens. In my backpack are Clif Bars I won't eat, a laptop, headphones, various nausea medications, and a sugarless orange Gatorade.

Ninety percent of the patients are elderly, all either bonneted up or having accepted the baldness. Whenever there's another young person here, we'll have a moment of solidarity upon noticing one another, a look that says *Yeah*, and then we'll turn back inward to our problems. I never talk to other patients. Dad will, though. He'll strike up chats, engage, talk about me. This is something we can never come together on. I will not be dragged into a conversation in this room.

Anyway, getting seated isn't the bad part, Dad's chatting isn't the bad part, even the toxic drugs aren't the bad part, not right away at least. The bad part is the IV.

I can't *just get* IVs these days. At some point in the hundreds and hundreds of IVs, it went bad or shifted into something psychologically problematic. The needles hurt now. Something about the IV, how the catheter sits there with its sharp plastic tongue in me. How I expect the chemo burning through my veins. How the muscles cinch up. Scar tissue on all the good veins.

The first nurse, in purple scrubs, is short haired, serious. He asks which arm we're doing today. I say left arm. He takes out a warm, wet towel and wraps it around my left arm. Heat and moisture help pop the veins out and bring blood to the area. I take some deep breaths, to prepare. Please be good, left arm, please obey. If you only obey, I'll do whatever you want. I'll do curls. I'll moisturize. For a time, I was left-arm-only for chemo, long months of just left arm. I think of these specific-arm times as eras. Left-arm era lasted for months. Then came a shorter era of right arm. But for the last two cycles, it's been back to left-arm-only. Now unable to even think about or consider right arm.

I'm sweating, every muscle tight, aware that this makes it worse.

The nurse lowers himself onto a spinning circular stool. He unwraps the wet towel. Arm hair has matted into curved patterns. With a gloved finger, he taps a vein on the underside of my left arm, then another, another. I ask him to please use a vein on the top of the arm, and he gives me a look, says, okay. *Tap, tap, tap. Tap, tap, tap.* He moves his head this way and that way to catch how the light hits my skin, to visualize the target. He finally picks his spot and says, "Try to relax." With his off hand he plucks the IV off the towelled tray. Tells me to breathe. Then the needle goes in, big sting. Sweat cascades down my back, my armpits. The needle still in, fishing around — breathe — back and forth, digging. I can't look. I close my eyes. *One, two, three, four.* Then hold. Exhale. *One, two, three, four.* Then diaphragmatic breaths, imagining grassy fields, focusing on my heart as a little white bonfire and each in-breath is all the black sludge of fear going into the fire and becoming purified until the fire again burns white. Seconds tick by, and he wiggles the needle through tissue and muscle, still looking, though I already know. He has missed. I wince, and he apologizes and takes out the needle. I nod. He says he can't find the vein. Beads of sweat on my face. He sees the beads. A black circle the size of a plum already at the needle site, blood under the skin, a deep bruise, black, then purple, then yellow. Two weeks to heal. I know all this already. It's always the same.

He smiles and acts cool, but he's nervous now about missing again. I don't know if it's my arm muscles contracting at the first feel of the needle in preparation for the pain, or a general fear, or whatever, but veins are getting harder and harder to hit. If I can't use the left arm and can't use the right arm, what do I do? It's a fucking problem. When I asked my oncologist to install a central line under my skin, the kind of IV that is permanent and can be easily plugged into, he said no, said he was worried about infection. And maybe he's right. Will the port fall out during sex, or weightlifting, or if I'm jostled? I don't know. Every other person in the ward has their central line running neatly from a raised disc of skin on their upper arm or clavicle, everyone except me, all smiling, their infusions simple and easy. I've had a central line before, for the stem cell transplant those years back during second cancer. It wasn't that bad, other than the cold feel of the tubes at night, and for this there wouldn't even be tubes because I wouldn't be hospitalized.

The nurse now feeling around my arm again, *tap, tap, tap*. Underside of my arm, no way, not happening. Move along, sir. Top of the arm, maybe. Can't be the hand, can't do it. Could be time to switch back to right arm? Left arm had a good run but is maybe now finished. Nurses missing all the time recently, the dread of it.

He asks where I want to try again, and I don't know. Where do we go? Where should I say to go? They don't like using the elbow crook because veins bend there and it's too far up the arm to go higher if that one also misses. I say lower down, different vein. He readies the needle again and goes in, top of the forearm. This one hurting twice as much. He's nervous for real. And it's my fault I guess, but it hurts so much, and why should I give a shit if he's nervous? We're both nervous, and both know he's going to miss again, that this is how our world must unfold. He digs around a while, the pain intense, and misses again. The needle goes through the other side of the vein, bursting it. Blood trickles from the injection site. He takes the needle out and does a big-cheeked exhalation. This bruise even bigger, blooming like a crop circle.

Dad sitting to the side through all of this, his face crunched.

The rule is, if you miss twice, you switch out. I didn't invent this rule, but it's an important one.

Several nurses huddle and whisper back and forth, then switch the guy out for a short red-haired lady. For switch-outs they usually grab the best nurse in the ward, the vein whisperer. The new nurse sits on the swivel stool and takes in the wreckage of my arm. The bruises growing like blast zones. She tells me she knows it hurts to keep missing, that she understands this is hard. We go to the right forearm now, on top, the big vein that skirts along the medial edge, you know the one. She goes in with yet another needle, slowly. It hurts, too, and takes longer than it should, but she gets the catheter in at last. Big breath. She flushes the line with saline to check flow. Tapes it down. The sting fading, fading, but still there. Saline always burns when it goes in fast. But it's done. I'm drenched in sweat. She clips the line to a saline bag and stands up to get the actual bad things going.

Before each drug, a nurse brings the bag to me — these bags themselves bagged and covered in warnings — and asks me my name and date of birth. Each time. Some godawful shit went on out east with chemo. Maybe Ontario. I can't remember. People getting the wrong dosage, watered down, later dying, families left to wonder if that was the reason. So now they check everything three times. Two nurses need to see my drugs, need to have me confirm that my name is on the drugs, before they'll inject them. These are good reforms.

She sets a timer on the IV pump and off we go. Chemotherapy infusions take hours. Infused too fast, these drugs melt veins. I don't talk much with Dad, though he asks how I'm doing or talks about the trapline or what's going on in Yukon. He knows I'm miserable and is just doing what he can, but I guess I'm an asshole on chemo days. I give one-word answers and look at my phone, at social media, at anything brightly coloured and delusional. Maybe I eat a weed edible at this point, though you don't want it to hit while you're still in the clinic — this not the place to be stoned. Ideally, the high comes just after finishing up, on the cab ride home, my forehead against the cool window, rain slick, watching the hedgerows and pastel houses in a blur.

I play loud rap music in my headphones and do breathing exercises where I imagine I don't have a head. Some of the drugs burn on the way in. I'm getting one of the MABs this time around, mixed in with the chemo. Monoclonal antibodies. Immunotherapy. Anaphylaxis is really the only dangerous side effect of these drugs; they're pretty great. This cycle, it's rituximab, but there's a bunch of them: brentuximab, durvalumab, nivolumab. This class of drugs basically allowing your immune system to do its job better. This is the future. They do the rituximab last, and have a nurse watch me to make sure I don't die.

With the chemo drugs, I feel them right away: heat, nausea settling over me, slow miasma, the way they make my skin want to fall off. In these chairs so much over the years; it's always the same. The drugs change, but it's always the same. I know these nurses. We age together. And when I get up from the orange chair, bracing against the armrest, and drag the IV pole to the bathroom to piss and my piss is the same colour as the orange Gatorade in my pack, it's also the same. I'm starting to realize that things follow and change shape as I change shape. No way to become a different category. So when the chairs are the same colour and the needles miss at the same location and the bruises spread into the same black nebula, *this* is the diversity and the uniqueness of experience. More and more it feels held in place by some external hand, though I wouldn't say God. Instead, I just think that I'm maybe getting what I expect, what I've always wanted, and that this will follow and will change as I change, however long this lasts.

•

THE OLDER ROOMMATE, THE ONE with dementia, moans and tosses around in his hospital bed each night. I keep waking, my pyjamas drenched in sweat, stuck to the bed. I limp into the shared bathroom and change into a new set of hospital clothes in the darkness, then go back to my bed and lie there listening to the old roommate as he writhes. I assume we all make these sounds at some point. Better I learn them now. The man's daughter is a nurse in the hospital, and she visits him before and after her shifts. He's a skeleton, disoriented during the day, mumbling, hand-fed by nurses. On the first day, he offered me five dollars to take him to the parking lot. Asked that I sneak him out of the hospital, please, five dollars, he's good for it, he's good for it. Later, yelling that he's in hell, in purgatory, to save him, to set him free. And I believe him. He's right. They use a ceiling-mounted sling to get him to the bathroom. The way his limbs puddle together like a stuffed toy as he's hoisted. He's always pulling out his catheter, the tube on the floor, golden rivulets tracing toward my corner of the room. Nurses losing patience. It's just hard. I can't help him. *Help* isn't the right word anymore.

After a few days of my not getting better, they are ready to drain the abscess.

I'm wheeled down several floors to the CT scanning room. I know this room. Dozens of visits here over the years. My radioactive age something like seventy-five. I've never had a surgical procedure *in* a CT machine before — how neat. I guess they'll be stabbing me in the pelvis and don't want to miss. What is the medically approved tool for stabbing? A stiletto? A screwdriver? My IV's already set up, so they hit me with the contrast dye, and the pissing-myself sensation comes on fast. I tell them I don't want to feel pain, that I'm anxious — these are the correct phrases to use, trust me. The doctor smiles and nods, takes out what I think is fentanyl and hits me with that through the IV. Okay, *okay*. Bye. Catch you later. Now off in a grey realm. Several hands grab and move me into a new shape. Distant pressure on my pelvis and spine. But all wrapped in a darkness that is not a dark colour. The CT scanner *whirs* to life, and this I can hear, its great vibration. I'm jostled, I'm pulled apart. Heat everywhere. They lance or puncture my low abdomen, maybe five inches from my penis, to hit the abscess. I don't feel it, but I'm aware. It's a mess. A release. I'm so high. Wet on my legs. I can't see. Something slides or is pushed into the puncture site. Then coming back down, teleported to the hallway. Nauseated.

The comedown terrible on this drug, and familiar from other times. Where is everybody? An empty hallway lit by buttery lights, halos at the corner of my vision. Waiting for an orderly. Dozing. A white tube sprouts from my pelvis now. There's a bag attached to the tube, the bottom full of orange pus, clouded white. More pus in the tube, moving visibly.

Things get better after they drain the abscess. A nurse comes each morning and squeezes pus from the hip tube into its dangling bag, then empties the bag into a bucket and brings the bucket somewhere unknown. The old roommate is heartbreaking at every point of the day. His daughter visits to talk with him, checks vitals, tries not to be his nurse, fails.

My sister Angela brings clothes from my apartment. She orders me Japanese food and meets the delivery driver in the parking lot. She perches on the end of my bed and tells me about grad school and working in a hospital ward for premature babies. Much better having her around. All the common knowledge, the understanding.

I'm still sweating so much at night that I need to change clothes at least once, sometimes twice, but the pain is down. Pus still fills the bag each day, and they track the volume. Only when I'm clearing less than fifty millilitres per day will they remove the drain. Skin puckers around the tube where it enters; it's gross and parasitic, the sensation, to have something in me. I'm on every antibiotic that exists and feeling awful.

The tall doctor comes in again and lets me know that they've discovered what bacteria was spreading through my blood — strep G, a canine variety. She's so pretty. I'm not at my best. Do I own a dog? No, I say. No dogs. Even my friends don't have dogs. The last dog encounter would have been visiting my parents up north two months ago. There's a look she gives, maybe deep down wondering if I'm some kind of bestiality guy. Or not. Maybe that's what I'd think if I were the doctor and that's why I'm not a doctor. Or I'm just imagining things and strep is everywhere, on our skin, our clothes, omnipresent.

When a resident finally comes in to remove the drain, she's accompanied by a more senior doctor from internal medicine. He guides her through it. Says to cut the internal wire in the tube, tug hard, and the whole thing should come out. It's not the first tube I've had pulled from me, and they are all disgusting. With body tubes you wish for a sanitized medical process to extract them, but all they ever need is a good pull. She's excited, this resident, loves wounds. I don't look. With scissors, she snips off the tape holding the tube in place where it exits my pelvis, then with some longer implement she severs the internal wire that keeps the tube pigtailed so it doesn't fall out.

"Pull hard," he says.

There's a *sloop* sound, a release of pressure, and then she's got this long tube in her hand, much too long, half of it crusted over with blood and tissue. They lower it into a biohazard container. He tells her to massage the entry site and squeeze out residual pus like toothpaste from a tube. So she does, her fingers around my hip, massaging, and I can feel more goo exit the puncture, though I still don't look. There's apparently a lot. She thinks it's cool, all this goo. And they wipe it away, wipe it away, disinfecting as they go.

Once everything is out, she slaps a bandage on it and says we are done. And I want to tell her no, we're not. I want to tell her this is an old story, want to say I've seen her before, been here before, half-asleep, in loose blue clothing, here where the lights never go out. But she already knows this, has leafed through my thick folio and seen the broad strokes, and concluded whatever it is doctors conclude. Likely not hopeful. Likely picturing a number in her head, the number drawn big and purple, the number until I won't have to come here anymore, to see everybody. The number until I won't have to tell them the story again, to toss and turn and hope the specific pain is gone by morning so I can again focus on the general pain. And it's not so much the pain, and it's not the hard beds or the needles; it's not even the fear of dying. There's just something to hospitals, like you're living inside the walls of a house, and there is a family living in the actual house, and you hear them and see parts of their lives through old nail holes where paintings used to hang, and feel the vibrations of their steps, but they never realize you're there.

•

I'm BACK IN HOSPITAL WITH a blood infection. At this point, I'm tired. I don't want the song and dance with the emergency room residents trying to figure out what's wrong with me. It's like being the guy at a party who keeps telling the same story to different groups, and eventually he gets drunk enough to tell it to the same group twice and someone mentions it, and everyone goes quiet. I tell them I already know what it is, but all the same questions come. Is it gonorrhea? Is it a hernia? Let's palpate the testicles. No, no, I say, please, it's not those things, it's the same strain of canine G streptococcus that it's always been. Please just give me antibiotics.

One of the doctors must have read my medical history, because he seems to believe me. They cart me up to a spacious room on the fourth floor. Nice digs at least. My roommate is behind a curtain, and they don't speak or make any noise. Later that night, Ronnie visits me, bringing various kimchi snacks and things I might need in a bulky canvas shoulder bag. Love is strange. Long relationships are strange. The comfort. The loss.

She calls these blood infections my "dog disease." It's partially a language barrier, but also hilarious. When she straight-faced says, "How is the dog disease?" I cannot stop laughing. She gets annoyed when I make light of these things, her lips going tight, and I can't figure out how to tell her that I *have* to make it funny, that it's how I survive. I imagine her texting her parents in Korea like, *Yes, he has the dog disease again. I hope he makes a swift recovery.*

But it might go further.

My sense of smell would be the first clue. A bit better than before. I'd be in my hospital bed, noticing scents that used to be undetectable — toenails, obligation, sunlight. Then it would progress. Hair would sprout in a ridge down my spine. I'd lose language, start communicating only in growls and yips. Run the halls on all fours, my IV pole trailing behind me on long, special cords for people like me.

She doesn't find the dog disease narrative funny, and frowns.

I pull her onto the hospital bed and kiss her. I've got a hospital shirt on and some sweatpants. And I can tell the antibiotics are working because of how my body reacts to her nearness. This is the only accurate metric for healing. She notices the neighbour's curtain and gets embarrassed, and I soon stop being a degenerate and we just sit on the bed and talk. Blood infections are small potatoes; she isn't worried, and why would she be? Ours isn't one of those situations where they ask, "But can their relationship survive the cancer?" No. The relationship was *born* in cancer, right from the beginning, and she chose to stay, and that means something, even if only that she's reckless. Or maybe they do still ask. Some questions never go away.

After an hour, she heads back to her apartment, and I bundle up for sleep. Hospital beds are so hard. The metal frame digs into my spine. I ask a nurse for extra wool blankets, and they arrive pre-warmed. I layer these over my legs and curl up in the glow of the IV stand. The light coming under the door reminds me of the Vancouver hospital, those weeks there, though it was seven years ago. Seven years is not long enough to get away.

In the morning they say I can go. I'll have to come back every day at 7:00 a.m. for antibiotic infusions, but that's so much better than staying. They'll leave the IV in and wrap it up with gauze mesh to keep it steady as I go about my life. Once again showering with a garbage bag tied around my arm, not easy to set up on your own. I have a roll of orange hospital tape that a nurse gave me a while back, and it works okay for adhering bags to your skin, though it always rips hair off. What I do is cut a bunch of six-inch strips and stick them to the edge of my bathroom counter. Then I wiggle my arm into the garbage bag and fold the plastic around and around until it's tight. I tape the bag's trailing edge around my bicep and add tape strips along the length of my arm to make a rough cast. Then I take the roll of tape and do a bunch of loops around the bag to make it as waterproof as possible. Some water always gets through, but as long as the IV port doesn't get too wet, it shouldn't get infected. Which, with all the antibiotics in me, probably isn't a big risk anyway. When I'm actually in the shower, I brace the taped arm against the wall to keep it out of the spray. This is tiring. I don't shower for long, or really relax. For the next week until they pluck the IV from my vein, this is what I do.

•

I WAKE UP WITH A sore left leg. It's only 6:30 a.m., still a half hour to the alarm, but the leg keeps me from falling back to sleep. I roll to one side, then the other. Rain patters against the window. I must have pulled a muscle at the gym last night, though I went to sleep feeling fine. Maybe a strain. Overuse, maybe, like always. After some eggs and water and vitamins, I get dressed and limp to the bus stop. I've been working for the government this past year, and it's better than nothing. The ride to the office is only a few minutes, and the leg only hurts when I move it.

As morning turns to afternoon, I clerk my way through stacks of paper. Only when I get up to make tea do I again notice the leg. The limp becomes a hobble, becomes dragging my left leg behind me like a zombie. Other people at the office start to stare when I pass by. *He showed up able to walk. What is his game?* The pain grows. But it's only when I begin to shiver that I understand. Ah. Okay. The blood infection again. Stupid of me not to have noticed in the morning, and now at work, far from home, no antibiotics in my bag. For some reason, I never notice the blood infection when it's *actually happening* but always think I've got the blood infection when I'm really just being a hypochondriac.

I've had antibiotics on me at all times for most of the last eighteen months, but don't have any at this exact moment in the office. I've been taking antibiotics whenever the old surgical site aches, as that is the sign of infection, but those other times weren't real, I don't think. Those other times were in my head. This one is real. The fever's speed is worrisome. I should really have noticed, waking up with the leg pain. Last time it presented in the exact same way: leg pain that wasn't there the night before, then almost unable to walk, then the shivering, wracked with chills, then the hospital.

I call the pharmacy. They can have the cefixime ready in thirty minutes. Good, good. I can still make it home without being too fucked up. Now, to try the new strategy. All the other times with the infection, I went to the hospital, and I don't want to go there anymore. The idea: get a strong oral antibiotic in my system as soon as possible following the onset of symptoms and, in this way, not have to go to the hospital for IV treatment. This approach is untested, and we don't know if the antibiotics are strong enough.

I tell my supervisor I have to leave, that my leg is infected. I don't talk about the chronic aspect, or the cancer. Just, leg infected, must go immediately.

I feel bad leaving my friend on the unit to do all the work. Working with these disability applications sucks. Every single one is cancer. Breast. Prostate. Lung. Brain. Skin. The whole human body in these stacks of paper, killing itself. Especially the terminal applications. They are bad even to accidentally look at or read words from. People with six months or less, who know it, whose doctor knows it to be so true they will put it in writing. Brutal. The letters. The stacks of medical information. All their treatments that I've also done, that I can taste and feel in my stomach, in my veins. I try not to read any of the work I process but must check the documents as part of the job. I keep glimpsing things. Seeing the names. Nuclear radiation readouts. Lists of prescriptions. Makes me dizzy and nauseated. Words like *effusion* leaping off the page. Words like *metastases* and *prognosis* and *staging*.

I can hardly walk with the leg but need to clear my desk before I leave. While dragging a stack of applications back to the main unit, I limp past one of the supervisors. She gives me a look like *How did you get to work?* It's funny. I try to imagine the thought process. If I witnessed a co-worker come into the office looking fine, and by noon they were limping so severely they needed a wheelchair, their face gaunt and sweating, what would I think? I'd need to ask. Would go crazy wondering.

Fever in full swing now, I try not to tremble. The infection so familiar and sudden. I call a cab and have them pull up right next to the building. I pour myself into the back seat, give the driver the pharmacy's address. We go, we are going. Time still for small talk. Time to not show worry. Once we get to the store, I ask that he stay in the parking lot with the meter running until I come out, trying to expedite things, trying to be smart. It'll be fast. I leave my bag in the cab to show good faith.

There's a long line of old people at the pharmacy. They're supposed to text me when my cefixime is ready. They haven't texted yet. They said thirty minutes, and it's been thirty minutes. Maybe forgot. Too busy. I move through the line balanced on my right leg, leaning on the little aluminum guardrail as I get closer and closer to the front. Twenty minutes later I say hi to the young man behind the counter.

He smiles and says that my order isn't ready. Says to wait off to the side and they'll call my name. Okay, sure. Wait off to the side. I make sure to clarify with him: So I should, like, lean here off to the side on one leg against the shelf of Christmas candy? Here off to the side, not in the line? And you'll call me to move ahead of the line when my order is ready since I've already waited in line? Just making sure. He says yes, off to the side, leaning against the Christmas candy, they'll call me.

I go lean against the shelf of buxom chocolate Santas.

But, very weirdly, everyone else getting rejected at the counter leaves to do other shopping, then comes back to wait at the back of the line. As I stand there, I get the text that my order is ready. Thank God. Now he'll call my name and I can move to the front of the line and get my life-saving drugs.

He doesn't call my name. He doesn't make eye contact at all. He moves his head *just so* behind a sign denoting no narcotics on site, so that I can't meet his gaze. And the line itself is impenetrable. This is not some library line or croissant-store line. This is a sick-person line. This is a line of people whose dicks are falling off. But I stand there, because he promised he'd call my name and I could go right to the front.

And soon, the person who was at the back of the line when I first stood off to the side has already been to the counter and left, and there is a new line of people, all as dour as the ones before.

The cab is still out front, my bag in the back, meter running.

Fever pulses through me. The heat, the cold. I wobble. Maybe I wasn't clear with the man at the counter. With extreme shame and slowness, I limp to the back of the line. We move quick at first, but the line slows to a halt when I'm in third position. A man and woman occupy the two counters. The woman is getting, like, ten different drugs, then asks if the counter lady will give her cashback — no, she won't, okay, that's fine, she was just wondering, it's never clear one way or the other about the cashback, but boy is it convenient, but she figured she should ask, but that's okay, she can always just mosey to the other checkout at the front of the store, where the people are pretty nice, and get cashback there, so don't worry about it. Then she's asking if they take such-and-such credit cards, and which of her medical insurances is covering this specific stack of ten prescriptions, or is it a combination of plans, each plan folding into the other plan's tender gaps in coverage.

The cab's out front still, engine humming.

The man at the other counter is asking about the drugs he's getting, how to use them, riffling through his wallet for a credit card, but oops, that's not the right one, how silly, that's his credit card for this other good or service, so he will just hunt through his five-inch-thick wallet for the right card; is it this card, no, not that one, how truly silly and foolish of him to think that was the card.

When I make it back out to the cab with my brown paper bag of medicine, the meter says fifty-six dollars. My three-block journey up the hill to my apartment shouldn't add too much to that. I don't tip.

I limp into my apartment and take the cefixime in the doorway. Some delirium now. There's a thermometer in the bathroom, also a couple Tylenol I knock back without water. My temp shows as thirty-eight. Not so bad. I can handle thirty-eight. I'm trying to do the math in imperial. I hop on my computer and research how long it takes for oral antibiotics to reach maximum blood-stream saturation. Juli is calling, worried. She thinks I should go to the hospital. I tell her no. It's fine. She doesn't have to come over and see me like this. A part of me wants her at a distance, in a place where she has *stories* of the bad things, but not so close as to be immersed in them. How do you protect against that without being alone?

I'm so cold my teeth clack together. I turn the thermostat to a number so high that it's location on the dial is dusty. You aren't supposed to use extreme heat to counteract the chills of a fever, so don't do this. I get under my duvet and pull it over my head. Only for a short while, I tell myself, just until I warm up. I slip in and out of sleep. Now so warm, everything liquid and murky. I put the thermometer in my mouth again. Thirty-nine point five. What is that? Like one hundred and three? I'm so tired.

Juli says she's coming over. Okay, babe, fine. Come witness, come behold. I limp to my apartment door and flick the lock so I won't have to get up to let her in. My phone buzzes when she arrives downstairs. Can hear her in the stairwell through the concrete. I'm melting, burning up. Need to escape the blankets or lower the thermostat or bathe in ice water.

She comes in with a big bag of stuff for me. She's worried. Why is the heat so high? Don't I know not to treat fevers with heat? Shouldn't I know more than anyone? She wants me to go to the hospital. No, no, no. Not the hospital. I tell her to consider a certain pandemic. And that if I go to the hospital with her and my temperature is a million degrees, we will *both* be considered afflicted, and things will get very tedious.

Yes, but if I am septic?

I say that if my temp goes to forty, we will go — *that* would be dangerous.

I take more Tylenol as she drapes a wet cloth on my forehead. I'm drifting in and out of a vacant half sleep, and apparently being funny, because she laughs hysterically from the kitchen and says she loves me. Always good when she laughs, pure and meant, and it's like all my countless years of *wanting* for people to laugh have now been focused into her, and this is the real reason to have practised so much.

She orders takeout pho. I'm not hungry but slurp down some salty broth to make up for all the sweating. My clothes are wet. Then we're on my bed, and she doesn't seem comfortable cuddling with me in my delirious state, like she'll hurt me, or something.

"It's okay," I say. "Come here."

And then we do cuddle. And every few minutes I take my temperature, the numbers coming back in the thirty-eight range, higher, then lower, then higher again.

"We should go to the hospital," she says. "We really should."

Again I tell her that I'll be okay, we can decide later. Later comes, and she again suggests. No, no. I'll be fine. Night arrives, though I don't know the time. More Tylenol. Water. An apple.

As we get ready to sleep, she flashes a nervous look. "Can I give you a blessing with my *abuelita*'s rosary?"

"Sure," I say. "Go for it."

So she grips the wooden beads in one hand, the cross swinging over my heart, and begins whispering. I can't hear what she's saying, and maybe it's in Spanish, so I wouldn't know anyway, or I'd only catch a few words like *padre* and *santo* and so on. I hope she's using the powerful blessing, not the middle-of-the-road blessing. By morning the fever will be down. I know it. It'll be down, and we'll be tired, as she won't have slept much in her concern, and I'll have tossed all night sweating into everything, the damp forehead cloth fallen to the side and crispy with salt. She'll have work, and her hair will be a big dark tangle, and the bass from the building's heater will rumble through the walls, and that will be my signal to rise.

•

I MEET JULI FOR THE first time at the local board game café. It's summer and the late-afternoon sun is a ramp of red light connecting the street and the sky. We are to play chess. I haven't played chess in years. I know how the pieces move, but I don't play. She shows up in a navy-blue dress and we get right to it on a roll-up board we find stashed below Monopoly and The Game of Life.

She checkmates me in three moves. I try not to act wounded, but quickly get another game going and apply maximal focus. This one goes better. I'm using too much time, but I eventually win.

I drink a beer. She sips a cider. I let her taste my drink; she lets me taste hers. She grimaces at the beer, a look that says she almost never drinks alcohol. I'm destroying the steel bowl of popcorn between us. Kernels go everywhere — they attack the knight, spill into my lap. I'm covered in butter. We aren't saying much, but it's comfortable. Talking only distracts us from the current position and the next move. I haven't met many women who want to win at anything as much as I do, but she's devious and driven over the chessboard. The most innocent face, but full of shenanigans with her queen. Sometimes she cracks into a grin when I avoid a calamitous fork or pin. Or she hums appreciatively. I like her sounds. Her hair is dark, held back with a multicoloured bandana. We are nervous.

We play for hours, resetting the board after each game without having to ask if we should continue. I have popcorn in my teeth. Around ten, I ask if she's ready to go, and she says she is. I walk her to her building, as it's kind of on the way to my own. Dark now, the city lit by condo windows. Hot wind off the ocean. Sky sweating moonlight. Her building is nicer than mine. New. Shiny. Mine trash in comparison.

"We should do this again," I say, not getting the vibe that anything else is in the cards tonight.

"Yeah," she says, "we should."

I've said the same thing before, but this time, I don't know, something about this time.

•

COUSIN JUAN DRIVES US THROUGH the desert in a new red SUV. As the highway curves out of Monterrey, yucca appear like scarecrows on the horizon. Juli lived here until junior high, until the phone calls started about paying for protection. Should be only a few hours to her uncle's house in Arteaga, a little town in the industrial heartland, among a mass of factories and warehouses. Cars, pens, robotics, chemicals — they make them here. These things must have been made elsewhere before. Soon, we begin passing through little towns demarked mostly by Oxxo gas stations and signs advertising cheap empanadas, all linked by industrial parks and big company logos.

The air catches in my throat and reminds me of Yukon.

I'm tired from the red-eye flight and lean against the cool window. Orange light suffuses the desert and mirages warble in the distance. I close my eyes, thinking of all the plane's passengers crossing themselves as we took off, doing so again as we landed.

Juan drops us off at the gate to Juli's uncle's, next to a long cream-coloured wall. He has places to go. Very gracious of him to drive us. Four hours driving a stranger. Families seem to work differently here: things are owed, obligations are real. The uncle's place takes up most of a city block. The walls are twelve feet tall, and the only way in is through a rusted metal gate that clanks and whirrs as it opens. All the nice homes have walls; it's very medieval. When I ask Juli why there is such a big wall, she says it's to keep out thieves. Are there thieves? I've never really had those ideas in my head before. I'd just use the term *people who steal things*. *Thief* makes me think of a person robed in black, a member of a guild, adhering to ancient scripture.

A twelve-foot wall isn't so impregnable, anyway. Even a poor thief could have a ladder. A tiny ladder would have me over that wall. Glass shards along the top? Throw a thick blanket over the glass. Clusters of spikes? A rolled-up rug. Concertina wire? I'd have to think about concertina wire. Some of the houses on this street have concertina wire, and its loops do look difficult to get over. Clippers might work, wire cutters. Or just being nimble, leaping, doing a flip. But what about dogs?

The house, all white stone, sits at one end of a broad courtyard of pecan and persimmon trees. On the opposite end is a small, tarp-covered pool. The driveway is a grid of big flat tiles, also white, and four white cars huddle in a row next to a set of sliding doors that go into the house. None of the cars are ostentatious — a Hyundai, a Toyota, two of the old VW Beetles Juli said her uncle restores as a hobby. Maybe advertising that you have money isn't a good idea in Mexico.

We go inside with our suitcases and meet Juli's aunt, everyone a bit nervous, me not understanding what they say. The place is freezing. I throw on a sweater and thick socks. No central heat in Mexico. Instead, space heaters, a fireplace, clothes. This must all be worth it in the summer, I assume.

Later that week, we walk to the town's Sunday market. At one corner of the park are two federal police cruisers and a man wearing a Darth Vader helmet directing traffic. The vibes are good. I'm the only non-Mexican in sight, but no one seems to notice. The park is ringed by stalls of locals selling tortillas and *champurrado* and toy guns and soda and sweet waffles. Beadwork. Clothing. Honey. It's all here. The sun beats down from a blue sky. I unzip my jacket to cool off, but a moment later am too cold. The temperature swings twenty degrees from one day to the next, and I keep making the wrong clothing decisions.

The marketgoers are a throng of cowboy hats and plaid shirts and Adidas sneakers. I haven't bought anything since I got here. After Christmas, maybe I'm just tired of the buying, and anyway, I don't have much money. Another cousin is with us as a guide, as a friend. He's kind and funny and seems like someone who keeps a lot tamped down inside. He is often speaking Spanish with Juli, and only sometimes do I get the gist of it. He buys a Styrofoam cup of *champurrado* from a stall near the eastern corner of the market. Looks like thick hot chocolate. Juli's been saying I should try it. I don't like sweets in general, but she says if it's good we should split one, as a cultural moment. Okay. Sure. Her cousin takes a sip, looks pensive. What does he think? He grimaces, says it's not a good *champurrado*, there will be other *champurrados*.

Evening softens the air as we walk. By morning it'll be almost freezing, but for now it's warm. As we leave the market, we pass more and more walled houses and compounds. Some of the walls are high and some are low, with many dangerous things affixed to their tops. You can go either way with walls: higher or more dangerous. Almost all the walls are smooth stone. No brick or wood. Nothing to hold on to or climb. Cars slip past electronic gates along the street, the gate always beginning to close the exact second the back bumper passes inside its radius. No good to have the wall open too long. Not like when the uncle lent me his car and I drove us around Saltillo for an afternoon in the sun and we visited art galleries and the city park where a man was singing, young couples on the benches, girls on laps, whispering. Not like how, when we got back to the house, I clicked the button for the gate while parking and then we sat in the car a moment, my hand on her leg, and then we stood in the dark courtyard, and I noticed the gate was still ajar. The button had not registered my finger's push. Tiny panic, hoping no one in the house saw. I returned to the car, cold night air against my neck, and fished the little gate controller from the cup holder. Then she and I walked to the open gate and I again pressed the button, right up next to the sensor to make sure the signal landed, and with a great creaking the two halves of the gate swung together, and we were once again in a place you could call *inside*.

•

I WALK BESIDE THE SLIMS River with a pack full of stones, the others just behind. The Yukon government has sent our youth conservation squad here via helicopter to repair a hike-in campground, and it involves moving stones from one place to another place. Sun cooks the valley floor. I shade my eyes with a gloved hand, the air almost sparkling with silt. The Slims River splits into a dozen threads across the flats, most narrow enough to hop. Silt coats everything, fills my mouth, my ears. I wake up in my tent each morning covered in what looks like ash, the stuff coming through tiny gaps in the zipper, silt in my pocket, silt in my eye. All carried on wind so loud I've been wearing earmuffs from the helicopter to sleep each night.

We leave the exposed valley and climb into a wooded area with camping sites. With a grunt, I pour my stones into the designated spot. I think the plan is to spread the stones out and make a hard, well-draining surface for a tent. This is a good location. There's wind cover here and places to tie tarps and hang food in trees so the bears don't get it.

Roxanne, Dave, Naomi, Mia — they all drop their rocks off and head back out with me, our now-empty packs looking like popped blisters. There's a conservation officer with us acting as chaperone and guide. He must be six and a half feet tall, sharp-nosed, his face a mancala board of old acne scars. He mostly keeps to himself, probably thinks this job is stupid. He does the chainsawing to clear new tent spots and oversees the shotgun. Maybe having him makes sense. In case the electric fences around our tents don't work.

As we traipse back into the wind for more stones, everyone squints. We are sunburned and unshowered, our hair caked with dust. The conservation officer follows at a distance, whistling.

Again we fill the packs with stones, and again we trek back to the camping area. We're almost at the treeline when someone says "Bear!" Maybe Naomi says it, maybe Roxanne. A grizzly, telltale back hump, jagged profile, has snuck up behind us. It walks in a zigzag pattern about fifty yards away, staring at us, then away, then at us, then away. The shotgun is locked up in the wall tent over the ridge. We all take out bear spray and flares. Chaperone guy fires off his flares first, and they careen and explode, the sound ricocheting off the valley's granite. The bear flinches with each blast, but it doesn't run. Two flares, three. We stand closer and closer together, magnetized. On the fourth flare, it turns and dashes into the trees.

I'm on a crew staking claims for my uncle's mining exploration company in north Yukon. Today working with Sean. We've stopped on a green slope to watch a family of bears play in the grass below. A mom grizzly and her two enormous cubs. The siblings roll and tussle like five-hundred-pound babies. I don't have my gun with me today. Sean's pump shotgun hangs off his shoulder on a braided strap I think he wove himself. He watches the bears through a small pair of black binoculars. I also do not have binoculars. Seems like the more days go by, the more things Sean has that I don't. He's better at this job than I am — I can be realistic.

The bears are a few hundred yards down the slope, the mom eating flowers as the kids play-fight. Sean watches them through the binoculars, his whip-thin body still against the backdrop of rock and sky. I'm perched on a boulder, looking over the green valley. The maps don't look so bad today, might be easy.

"Should we go?" I ask.

Sean nods, fitting the binoculars into a little pouch. "Yeah, let's go."

While taking the luggage upstairs, I pass my brother's childhood bedroom and see the rifles. Looks like Dad's .270 and a 28-gauge, leaned up against the wall next to Alex's old books and Game Boy games. Guns are never just *lying around* our house, so I am wondering. I drop the suitcase off and go back downstairs. Dad's outside working, as always, a bucket of liquid fibreglass at his feet, the boat on sawhorses.

"What's with the guns upstairs?" I ask.

He doesn't stop. "Been some bears in the neighbourhood. Judy down the road saw one."

Okay. I go back inside, still wondering. There are bears all over, but I've never seen guns leaned up against the wall like this. They're trigger locked, but I still haven't seen it. Where's the ammunition? If it came to that, I'd want to know where. I'll ask him later.

Jess's kids are playing in the yard now, Aoife and Niamh, both under five, running around. Dad is protective of them; we all are. I'm thinking now of last year, Dad's friend, the guy he'd been teaching to trap and be a bushman, his protege, really, more than I ever was or could be. That protege got married to a nice French lady in town and they moved out into the bush to trap and live off the land, like he'd always wanted. They had a baby. Her picture is on our fridge. And one morning in early winter, he went to check the traps and came back to a bear standing over their bodies. When the bear tried for him, too, he shot it, and it died, and it was over. That picture on the fridge, the guns against the wall — I understand and don't need to ask about it again.

Upstairs with Juli, I hear a sound and stop folding clothes. On this property, I know all the sounds: crows, dog barks or howls, wolf howls, songbirds, thunder, mosquitoes, my dad on the chainsaw or the axe or the circular saw or the drill or the compressor. This sound is different.

I go downstairs to the entry, as its window has the best view of the yard. A massive black bear is half-inside the old chicken coop where my dad stores garbage and recycling.

Dad's been warned not to have the garbage in there, but it's not so easy to avoid. No garbage pickup outside city limits. You need to drive your own garbage to the dump. Which he's not going to do every day.

The bear finishes tearing the wall apart, grabs a bag in its mouth, and trundles back into the trees.

Juli comes downstairs and I tell her about the bear. She runs upstairs.

I make sure the front door is bolted.

Mom is at the desk in her office, working, soon to retire from the nursing program at Yukon University. I tell her about the bear. She looks worried but says it should be fine, that I should call the conservation officer hotline.

Back in my brother's room, I appraise the gun situation. Where are the bullets? There's a wooden box on the carpet next to a crate of wool sweaters. Inside is an array of munitions.

I haven't fired a rifle in years and want to look like I know what I'm doing.

One by one, I check the guns to see what calibre they are and how they load. There's the scoped Remington .270 my dad hunts moose with — his favourite — that loads via a small magazine. Next is the old 28-gauge I remember firing at willows when I was twelve. There's a rusty .30-06 in the corner. Big calibre, bolt action, open sights. Very old, though, and single shot. No shotgun in the pile, which is what you want for bears. The bullets in the box, strangely, are mostly shotgun slugs. That and racks of empty .270 shells that need to be reloaded. I find a single .30-06 bullet, which I palm.

A black plastic case leans against a bin of my sister's clothing. I open this up to reveal a compound hunting bow with pulleys and gizmos all over it. This must've been a gift from one of the Québécois guys my dad guides on moose hunts; they always arrive with all kinds of crazy shit. I close the case, just as likely to shoot myself with it than anything. Maybe I can arm Juli and make her into *The Hunger Games*.

In the far corner, I find another bow, this one an old recurve I remember from childhood, though I don't think I've ever fired it, either.

Juli is giving an excited or frightened play-by-play from the other window. "There it is, it's back. No, now it's gone. Now, it's back. It's eating compost!"

I go watch. The bear is on its belly, stretched out, head and shoulders inside a fifty-gallon barrel of compost. Might be a while.

I need to choose my weapon. The .270 seems best and has bullets, so I shoulder it and go downstairs. The magazine holds six shots, but I only put in four. I balance the rifle on the meat freezer in the entryway. Ready for war, I call the conservation officer hotline. They answer, bored with all the bears they hear about, say to hold tight, someone will be out.

I try to explain to Mom how the .270 works. Like, should I die, you'll need to send a hailstorm of lead at the bear. This is the safety, this the magazine, and all that. I don't think she's paying attention. She's stressed. I get it. We can't all keep a cool head.

Eventually, the CO's truck pulls into the driveway. He parks halfway down, opens the door, but stays behind it like in a stand-off. Must be applying mosquito spray. He soon comes onto the deck and knocks, only half facing the door, one eye on the woods. Young guy in a tactical vest, all kinds of tools in pouches. I let him know the general direction the bear went. He says he'll go have a look around.

Ten minutes later, he's back. I go out to talk. Mosquitoes hit us in clouds.

"So, where's Jacques?" he asks.

Must know Dad from somewhere. Everyone wilderness-adjacent in Yukon knows Dad from somewhere. With the trapping, with his working for the Department of Fisheries for twenty-five years, going up and down the rivers, with how he is.

"He's out at the lake."

"Still storing his garbage, I see."

He's not wrong, but I feel like defending the garbage storing. "Guess so."

He scuffs his black boot against a deck plank. "Couldn't find the bear. He's strewn shit all over the woods. We have to clean it up."

I'm nodding.

"Anyone in the house who can help should help." He keeps an eye on the woods.

"Give me a second." I don't think anyone inside wants to help. I throw on track pants, an old shirt, an even older sweater overtop for the mosquitoes. There are stained gardening gloves on the wood box, and I scoop those up. I mist myself with the mosquito spray we've been using on my sister's kids, the one with no DEET that doesn't work.

Back outside, I tell him it'll be just us.

"I have to watch for the bear," he says, shaking his head sagely. "You'll have to do it." He reaches into his pocket and pulls out a pair of black nitrile gloves. "Here."

Off we go behind the shed. The bear has taken several bags of garbage and torn them apart across the shrubs and willows.

"I went to school with your sister," says the officer as I kneel to pick up some empty juice boxes.

"Angela?"

"Yeah."

"Oh, cool. She lives in Dawson now."

"I heard that."

The first pile of garbage is mostly sawdust. But there are premade-coleslaw bags, yogurt containers, Styrofoam meat trays, oily plastic wrap. I stuff everything into a big black garbage bag. Then do the next area, a bit to the right. I'm sweating and eating mosquitoes with every breath. There's the sense I'm being demeaned, dealing with the garbage while he stands there with the gun.

We move to the overturned barrel of compost next to the greenhouse. The stench hits at about five feet. I stop. My sense of smell is terrible, but bile rises in the back of my throat at superspeed. Can't use my hand for this. I look around. One of the old shovels leans against the woodshed. This old shovel has been here for decades, the haft split in places, the blade rusted over. I get to work scooping and pushing rancid slop into the barrel. Then I pull the barrel upright and shovel in the spilled-on soil as well. Try to get all the slime. I start to gag and back off, heaving. After a minute, I get back to it.

The officer says all attractants need to go into the trapping shed, as its door has a crossbar. The barrel of slime weighs fifty pounds. I drag it one-handed, trying not to let any liquid that's spilled down its side brush onto my pants. Lifting the barrel into the shed is harder still, and the guy doesn't help, is still focused on guarding us. I stuff all the garbage bags in, the small shed already putrid — Dad might not be overjoyed. As I'm doing this, the guy gets another call about a bear down the road. Same bear? New bear? Who knows? We say our goodbyes. He'll come back later with a bear trap. Fine, good. I traipse back to the house, tired, and strip all the clothes in the laundry room. After a quick shower, I go upstairs, where Juli is still at the window, looking out. I pull her into a hug and let her know there's nothing to worry about.

•

I KEEP SEEING THIS GUY downtown. In the afternoons, in the evenings, I see him walking on various sidewalks near Douglas Street, near my office. I know him. We used to work at the deli together. He arrived only a few months before I left, but I remember. He's tall, this guy, with big shoes that kind of look cartoonish because of how his feet reach way ahead of his body as he walks. He's always wearing black clothes. Maybe late thirties back then at deli. No idea his age now — how do years work? But I've been seeing him so often, walking around. When we pass each other, he never indicates that he recognizes me. I try for eye contact or a head nod, but there's no recognition. I've had many recent medical appointments, which force me to leave my job early and catch buses this way and that way in the afternoon, which is when I see him walking around, so maybe he's looking for a job.

I remember when this guy started at the deli. Came in like a hurricane. Always busting his ass, a little paper notebook in one big hand to jot down reminders to himself. This enthusiasm pissed off the long-term employees, as you can imagine. Motivated, right?

No one likes a motivated co-worker when they are already ashamed of their menial work. I wanted to tell him to relax, wanted to tell him he wouldn't be rewarded. But I never did. I just kept my head down when we were on shift together and did my work with a fake smile for the customers wanting meat, and one shift blended into the next.

He'd talk to me sometimes about his plans. Said he'd been going to school but had to take a semester off to work and save money so he could afford more school. Then that semester off turned into another semester off. Hard to make ends meet, you know? And now here we are, ten years later? Fifteen? Swallowed whole. Minimum-wage jobs have a way of infiltrating hope. They keep you just above poverty, a dollar away, striving for that raise, for the gold name tag or the shift supervisor hat with a slightly larger apple on it. And he was all the way in it. So every shift we worked together, he'd be half jogging to the freezer, arms overflowing with boxes of frozen cookie dough, sweat on his brow, toiling. I'd be there, like, *This is unnecessary.*

And eventually, yeah, he got made shift supervisor, though he didn't get a special name tag, just a stickered title below his name. Two dollars more an hour, or so went the whispers among us other employees hunkered behind the cutting table stealing bites of egg salad and cookies and salami like he never would. Two whole dollars more per hour. Which made him more annoying, but also more tragic. How, when you glimpse that slight advancement, the hunger renews and you take another semester off, and then another. He talked about being let go from his last job after grinding up the ranks for years. Of course.

Around that time I was trying to exit, having realized that I could not continue being this poor. I kept seeing the word *under-employed* skywrite itself across my mind as I spooned gooey olives into clear plastic display jars — black olives, cheese-stuffed olives, and these little green ones that looked like Granny Smiths. What a bullshit term: *underemployed*. But here I was, my family all making good money back in Yukon with their government jobs, *buying things* when they wanted to. A real trip, menial work. Pulls you right in. Fresh out of grad school, teaching up the hill at the university, I wasn't immune. Next thing you know, you're working random shifts, with your weekends on Monday and Tuesday, and you think it's fine. You'll put your head down until they give you Tuesday and Wednesday as your weekend, and that'll be pretty great, right? That is the progress now. And this new guy who'd just been made shift supervisor, he was coming in at the tail end of my realization of what had been happening to me for three years. But three years is nothing. People do ten, people do thirty-five. Folks with good jobs have no fucking idea what goes on.

But I've been seeing him a lot recently, walking around downtown, always in the kind of black outfit you can wear in a kitchen, a deli, a grocery store. Now remembering how he'd talk about the concept of moving up and getting a paycheque that was one thousand dollars. As a dream, this cheque size. At the time, I wasn't getting thousand-dollar paycheques either, obviously, but I knew not to have that as the target. Not in British Columbia. Not in Canada. Get real, you will be eaten alive.

By the time he got assistant manager, I was out of there, hired as a dishwasher up the hill, making almost twenty dollars an hour because of the university's union. Still a bad job, covered in refuse and half-eaten food, but money wasn't so tight anymore. The cheques crept over a thousand dollars.

I see him walking with his head down and it all comes back. The countless days making salads and selling razor-thin prosciutto and the brutal customers who don't like the harried or exhausted expression on your face and complain to the store owner, and you get roasted later and written up and don't know what you did wrong. Buckets of mayonnaise going into every goddamn thing. And this guy most certainly still in that swamp. He must be, seeing his face. No affect there at all, how he can be both facing straight ahead and turned away all at once. I'm sure he's not at *that* deli anymore, because eventually, at all these places, the managers who've been there fifteen years can't afford to pay you any more than the dogshit they already do, so you are stuck and upset about it, and they know, and you know, and you just have to go or you're forced out. But he's somewhere. Or, like I suspect, between jobs.

You don't ever want to be between jobs at this level. That is the danger zone. That is being one missed cheque from eviction for a lot of people. I never had to be in that zone, could always get money from back home if I needed it — and often I did — but I've worked with a lot of people in that zone. That zone is a palpable vibration that comes off them. Going around with a little folio of resumés, ten pages of kitchens and restaurants and Home Hardware.

I don't know what I can do for this man. He doesn't see the way out, and maybe there isn't a way out. Maybe all this shit was set in motion because he didn't have parents who could give him money, and that's just the end. Maybe there was never a chance he'd finish that semester and dodge these kitchens and walk-in coolers where dead pigs sway in the breeze of fans and every plastic container has a label made from masking tape and black Sharpie. Every time I see him walking, I want to look at the bottoms of his shoes. I'd see all the built-up food in the soles, the gristle and bone and vegetables, and at least get a sense of where he's been and what's going on. But he won't recognize me, I know, no matter how often we pass on the street. He won't look up. He won't nod. There's something that stops this from happening, something that makes it impossible.

•

I TAKE THE ALOE PLANT off my bookshelf and place it in the bathtub. It's time. I've had this aloe for five years, and now it's too big and asymmetrical and going to fall over. My tiny apartment doesn't have a patio, so the plant only gets light from one side, and its limbs reach so far that when I push on the pot, the whole thing wobbles and threatens to fall. I've been taking scissors to the plant's limbs and amputating any arm that reaches too far toward the light. Yellow aloe spills from the severed stump, and I need to keep dabbing at the opening with a paper towel like a combat medic. The plant looks brutalized but will not die. One time, as I sat watching the aloe drip in a long string from a newly cut area, I even began to wonder what it would taste like, the goo, so I tried some. Foul beyond belief, the bitterest thing I've ever tasted.

Now, this big aloe has started to grow little children alongside itself — I think they're called pups. There are two of these pup aloes. Unlike their mother, they have many leaves instead of the few big strong ones. I think I'm meant to cultivate them through pruning, cutting off leaves until the remaining ones learn to grow thicker, dominant.

My bathtub is where any plant stuff has to happen. There isn't anywhere else. The tub itself is a bit sketchy. On the outside of the tub wall there's an indentation, and under that you can see a bright-red line of rust. It looks like one tub was placed inside a larger tub, instead of just replacing the larger tub. I've never asked the landlord if this is the case, if my small bathtub is resting inside the cadaver of an older, completely rusted bathtub, but I don't know what else it could be.

Anyway, I've got this giant amputee aloe in the tub, and an empty ceramic pot. I kneel on the linoleum and start to dig soil away from the base of the aloe. I'm looking for the root stem. I try not to get too much soil in the tub, because it's hard to get it down the drain and I need to use my hands to push it through the grill,

which I don't like doing, as the grill has a lot of hair and other un-
knowable things in it. I don't want to cut too far down the plant's
body, but I also don't want to cut too far up. I've got my little red
paring knife in one hand. Two inches down the stem, green transi-
tions to brown and the texture goes coarse. Okay, good. I take the
knife and saw through the thick green tissue until the plant comes
away from its own root system. I pull the big aloe out and put it in
the other pot, where I've already placed a few inches of soil. Now,
the pot has just the two pup aloes and a big crater where their mom
used to be. I drop in some volcanic stones I ordered online that are
apparently fertilizer and fill the crater with soil mix. I tip the soil
bag into the second pot and fill it as best I can, making a huge mess
in the tub. Soil all over the place, in my hair, down my shirt. I hope
the little aloes live. I hope the big aloe lives, too.

I'll leave the little aloes on the bookshelf nearer the window
and sunlight. The big one I'll move to the coffee table, next to the
begonia, and hope that's good enough. It'll be obvious in a day or
two whether it will die or not. Plants communicate what's going
on with their bodies — they don't dissemble about their own sorry
states the way people do.

•

I GAIN TWENTY POUNDS DURING the R-CHOP chemother-
apy. Like everything, the treatment eventually ends, and I'm left
with the summer to collect myself. *Some* of the weight might be
muscle, but I'm not sure. Even small workouts leave me gasping,
but I persist — squats in front of the bathroom mirror, laboured
walks through windstorms wearing three sweaters, walks back
from follow-up blood tests, aimless walks to nowhere. The steroids
inflated me like crazy, but in time they, too, begin to pass from
my body.

A low-level agoraphobia fills me. Maybe it's more than just being bald and ghoulish and feeling ugly. Deep down, I'm hoping
to teleport through this. Everyone's so disconnected, I can go
through a whole cancer, multiple cancers, and friends might not
even know. This feeling like if they don't remember, I won't remember. Especially if we don't live in the same city, or if they're busy
with work, or now with kids. I'm not documenting medical dramas
on social media, so when it's finished, if I'm alive, I can go back to
Yukon for a visit like nothing happened. I'll go to parties and see
everyone from high school, and when they ask me how I'm doing, I
can lie and think I'm telling the truth. They don't know how many
times it's been now, and I don't blame them.

The baldness isn't terrible. My skull lacks big dents or dinosaur-
like geometries, anyway, but I still don't like it. After a few months,
peach fuzz sprouts across my head, though now there seems to be a
bald spot that wasn't there before, which is awful.

I try to work out as my energy returns, try to eat out less. Ronnie
sometimes pokes my belly and says it's sticking out, and I want to
be like, *I love you. Are you fucking kidding me?* But instead, I try to
laugh it off. Maybe that's just how they talk to each other in Korea.
She says her mom is always suggesting she get a nose job, or that
she's fat, or this or that. Either way, for all her great attributes, her
poise and curiosity, those physical comments don't feel good.

The relationship to body can't ever be the same after one cancer, let alone three. I understand that now. Each day as I recover,
I worry about it coming back. That first relapse, when I suspected
it was back and no one believed me, was a bad thing. Being right
was awful. Wish I never suspected, never said the words. Now,
the hypervigilance spirals out of control. I tell myself not to even
attempt magically noticing cancer, but I'm on high alert all day. It's
not healthy for some things to feel possible. So crucial to let go of
knowing when it will come back. At some point it will be obvious

that the cancer is back, and all the months and years imagining it's back won't have been useful. I say this and say this and say this.

I need to be oblivious again. I need to do less. Need to do so little, not even use my muscles, go down to the level of bone, be a marionette. Be like that time in kindergarten when one kid in our class disappeared and we didn't know what had happened to him. Then, one day, he came back to visit us in a wheelchair, totally bald. I was five and didn't understand. They said he was very sick. Leukemia. Leukemia and the bisected age groups, how it hits children. Blood cancers do that. Young or old, they will come. I don't think I was very good friends with the kid, or even with anybody not in my family at that point. Do five-year-olds have friends? Or was I a loner? But this kid with leukemia, he visited the class for a single afternoon after having been gone for so long. Skin so pale. The noises coming from the chair. They always say children handle cancer more nobly than adults, and I'm sure he did. I don't know if I said anything to him, just gathered around with all the other kids who gathered around. And at the end of the day, off he went, the visit over. Soon after that he died, and that was my first memory of someone being sick and not getting better.

•

I DRIVE JULI OUT TO my parents' place on the shores of Crag Lake. Our romantic getaway. As I turn off the highway onto the dirt road into the woods, I get the sense that being out here might be unsettling for her. To be driven far into the woods after a life in cities. Such a secluded property, away from everything and everyone — maybe that's what my father wanted. The driveway is a long road off another long road, sinuous in the way of paths made by a single person. They've poured gravel over the driveway to give it shape and keep the forest back, but you can only do so much out here. Grass and fireweed already reclaiming. Small willows at the edge, one toe across the line. All the trees are old and marked by burls, this region overdue for a burn. Not sure why there are so many burls on the trees in this patch. Malignancies prove they're alive, I guess.

Before bed, I go around putting pillowcases over the windows. The upstairs is so bright in the summer. Midnight sun. Five a.m. dawn. No rest. There are curtains, but they are a sheer green gauze meant for winter. I remember the countless trips Dad took to build the place. Gone weeks and weekends. Always loading material into his truck. Must've taken more than twenty years. I didn't help much, always begging off, busy. At some point, he even bought the land, though I'm not sure how. Since it was originally a trapping cabin, a bit of zoning magic might have come into play. Trapline law is archaic and difficult to conceptualize. There's still a wall tent in the bush at the back of the property where he used to stay, even in winter, while getting the foundation in. He milled the wood himself, framed it himself. I'm so much less useful. What an endeavour. He'd bring in friends or family in the trades for the stuff he didn't know. His brother, Andre, the stonemason, for the tile and concrete. A gang of other ex-patriots from Quebec, I'm sure, for the carpentry, the electrical.

Funny that someone like my dad, who hates the slightest noise while trying to sleep, built a house that amplifies every sound. Can hear a whisper from the basement to the third floor. The woods being so quiet makes it worse. No car noise, no electrical humming, nothing beyond songbirds and wind. I've stayed here by myself to write and gotten so freaked out at night I had to check all the locks.

The top level is open concept and made of pine. Pine framing on the windows. Pine trim. Pine floors. There's a big painting on the wall by Halin de Repintigny, this artist from Dawson — white mist in the air, a birchbark canoe full of *coureurs des bois* surging

through rapids, their faces jubilant and focused. My dad traded
firewood for it in some exchange, like he's always doing. There is no
bedroom on the top floor, just a bed in the middle of the space and
two foam mattresses up against the wall. We're a big family, after
all. Not to mention my dad is always inviting people we don't know
to come stay — trapper friends, random folks he meets at the store,
hitchhikers — which drives my mom up the wall. The sleeping ar-
rangements often more like camping indoors. When we're all here
at night, you hear everyone go up and down the stairs for water or
the bathroom. Each creak and step as if it were inches away. Each
voice and exhalation so close. And I kind of like it. He built our
childhood home, too, so it's always been like that. You get used to
it, the closeness of people, of knowing where they are, when they
come, when they leave, and that's what I miss when I'm not here.

•

I PULL ONTO TAGISH ROAD and head east toward Atlin. Juli's
in the passenger seat, her eyes on the forest. There is no end to the
trees and lakes and mountains — Yukon is bigger than Germany,
but with fewer than forty-five thousand people. Heat waves curl off
the road ahead. Another hot day, blue-skied, gentle wind through
the pines. Dust clouds swirl in the old Subaru's wake as I get into
third gear. This whole section of road is currently gravel, and the
tires roar against it, the vibrations travelling up my legs like I'm in
an airplane that's just landed.

I want to roll the window down but don't because of the dust. I
keep the car below seventy, both hands on the wheel. I don't want
Juli more concerned about the Mad Max vehicle situation than she
may already be. I'm being harsh — the Subaru's in *okay* shape. Dad
said he just put a bunch of money into it, new struts, timing belt,
that kind of stuff. I'm thinking the car's from 2004. Juli interjected

a few days ago that "the windshield looks very post-apocalyptic," which, with her slight Spanish accent, had me dying of laughter. Our windshields have always been so fucked up, I hadn't even noticed. Back in high school, my beater Honda's windshield was one big spiderweb. Living out of town, we were always on the Alaska Highway, a major trucking corridor, and trucks throw rocks. Makes no sense to fix the glass every single time. For us it was a question of *Can I see through the glass?* and if the answer was yes, or even somewhat, then the windshield was okay.

Around the next bend, there's a bear in the ditch. I slow down, then stop. A small black bear the colour of chocolate, eating flowers. Probably its first season alone without family, always the hardest one. The bear doesn't react to the engine, though we're so close. It continues to eat flowers, sniffs the air, throws a sidelong glance. We sit and watch it for some minutes — they are beautiful sometimes, like everyone.

But we have places to be, so I hit the throttle and keep going.

The right side of the road is one lake after another. The left side is mountains, hard brown rock, jagged cliffs. Heat builds up in the car as we go. I wipe my brow with my shirt collar and take a sip of water. The air conditioning doesn't work, try as I might with the knobs.

I put a hand on her thigh and squeeze. She leans across the seat divider and rests her head on my shoulder. Nice to be on the open road, driving from one lake to another lake. Every day should be this day. We could visit all the lakes in the world. Or find two perfect lakes and go back and forth between them. Whatever we chose would be perfect.

Forty minutes later we pull off onto another gravel road, take another left, then enter a tunnel formed by willows. This isn't even a road, just a place where the willows have been cut. Sound dies off. Dense forest, riparian. The tunnel opens onto grass. My family's sixteen-by-twenty cabin appears. Dad is addicted to building cab-ins; he will never stop. My aunt's yurt is across the way, though I don't think she stays there much anymore, after an incident where she went to grab the door handle and her hand closed around a bat instead. The other family we share land with, the Emonds, also have a yurt half-visible through the trees, and I see Diane on her knees in the garden, busy as always.

The soil is a rich black, and the garden at the far edge of the property bursts with potatoes and carrots and broccoli in neat rows. Mosquitoes fill the air like a fine mist and bounce off the windows. Sun coats the field. I can see my brother's car next to the old picnic table. Red and blue coolers stacked up near the fire. Food on the go. There's such a heart feel to arriving here. Done it hundreds of times and it's always good. How you break from the trees and see the firepit and the picnic tables and the grass going on and on, and the feel never changes, might be the only stable thing.

"This is it," I say, not sure how to express the importance. How do you put childhood into so few words?

We hop out and dose ourselves with bug spray. Juli's been get-ting eaten alive. Swollen red hives the size of poker chips mar her legs and back and shoulders. I don't get marks from mosquito bites, which is nice. They bite me but leave no red dot or itchy swelling. I spray her down as best I can but know it won't make a huge dif-ference unless we get the real poisonous stuff, and I don't want to do that.

The fire's burning low and its smoke traces skyward in a thin stream. Our families have always kept a cinder-block firepit near the creek side of the property. The fire going for days at a time, stoked by us children up late, fed by my father up early. I smell burgers and char and oil. Several dogs race around.

I grab a cup of water from a big blue jug and pass it to Juli. Alex and his girlfriend, Lish, must be down at the shore or swimming.

I go into the old kitchen shack and change into my swimsuit. The shack has an immense old table where we play board games. Ragged foam mattresses are stacked against the wall, and there's an ancient wood stove in the corner that we never use. Whenever I'm in here, I think about the time we found a chickadee in the stove. It had gotten trapped in the chimney when we weren't there and died from starvation or breathing in old ash, or both. Dad said he could hear the bird's mate singing and looking for it for days.

I show Juli around the property and tell her where the outhouse is, though she's said she will not use one. Grabbing a bag of bug spray, sunscreen, and towels, I lead her to the warped bridge that crosses the creek. Wild rose and raspberry choke the path. Thorns everywhere. Too late, I tell her to be careful. Red line down her calf, not so bad, she'll be okay. Mosquitoes and flies cloud the air. We get through to the old road between our property and the neighbour's place up on the hill. From there it's a short stroll to the dock. Several boats bob in the water, and there's an old sink station for gutting fish. There's even a new plastic extension on the dock. No Alex, though. No Lish. They must be at the other end of the property, where we keep our fishing boat and canoe. The dock planks swell up and down under our feet as we walk out. Half the dock is submerged and buckling, the old thing way past its prime. Reaching the end, we hold hands and look over the water.

I strip to my swim trunks and put my glasses and phone in the tote bag. She's already got her bikini on. I lather her back with sunscreen, kiss her neck, wrap her in a hug. She gets my back next, though it takes longer. Then we stand still for a moment, like anyone does before entering cold water. She dives first, fast, like she hasn't heard that you're meant to delay jumping in. Not a bad dive. I haven't seen her swim yet, but she looks comfortable in the water, and it makes me happy. She surfaces with a little shriek and paddles away into the deeper blue. Now, I have to jump in, no choice. I leap.

The immersion takes my breath away. I surface and swim after her. We laugh and shiver, gleeful with cold. I do some breaststroke, trying to remember how, then circle back. There's a metal truss on the end of the dock about two feet below the surface that works as a slimy step to climb out. I drag myself from the water and shake off. Juli places a foot on the truss; I grab her hand. We wrap ourselves in towels. I'm kissing her ear when I hear voices. My brother's lanky form passes from the trees, Lish just behind, her stride and energy always so determined.

They ask how the water is. We say good. They want to swim at the other end of property, and they have water toys. So off we go, back through the thorn path. Juli gets bit, like, fifty times by flies and mosquitoes along the way. Soon, we're skittering down the sandy path to the abbreviated shore at the property's south end. There's a small kayak, a full-size stand-up paddleboard, and a Canadian Tire inflatable doughnut. Juli and I sit on the paddleboard, and I push off the shore. There's only one paddle, so it's slow going. Alex is in the doughnut, making big scooping motions with his arms. Lish, clearly experienced, zooms ahead in the kayak. The water is shallower here, five feet, six feet. I paddle us farther and farther from shore. My feet get cold as the water deepens and goes a shade of blue-black. So beautiful, pollen slicking the surface like yellow oil. No one else out here. Even the mosquitoes can't follow. A gentle wind picks up and dries my shoulders. The sun moves beyond the last few clouds into open sky, and it is warm again. I want to hold the moment in my cupped palms.

Juli slides off the paddleboard and swims away. "The water's so nice," she says, body pale against the blue.

Lish says she wants to try the paddleboard, so I slip into the water too. I float, held. Warm near the surface, cooler around the legs. Juli and I swim circles; I show her my rendition of the butterfly. Everyone laughs, but I swear it's not bad. We rest a while with our elbows on the paddleboard, still mostly in the water, and it feels like home. Why not live here, in the water? We'd acclimate. We'd grow scales. I swim away again, front crawl, trying to go fast. I'm shivering but don't want to leave. Juli's swimming next to me. We try to embrace while treading water, her legs wrapped around my waist, and sink immediately. A moment of darkness, then back to the surface. We sputter and laugh. I blow water out of my nose. She shakes her head, long hair whipping around.

I take a turn in the kayak, then in the doughnut. They all say I should try to stand up on the paddleboard, so I climb on. The board rocks wildly as I get to my knees, then my feet.

"Look at the horizon!" shouts Lish as I pitch over and go under.

I try again and don't even make it to my knees before face planting into the water. Even I'm laughing at this point. If only I could look at the horizon. My back's getting sore, but it's so funny. I try again, face plant again. Once more, again falling over right away. Not going to happen. Breathing heavily, I straddle the paddleboard and help Juli climb on for a break from the water's cold. Something zooms through my peripheral vision. A horsefly has followed us. Juli shrieks something about how they are her phobia, and dives into the water. I swing the paddle around, trying to kill the horsefly, but keep missing.

Dad is on the shore with his bloodstained tacklebox and life-jackets, prepping the boat. He asks if we're okay, if it's fun, if it's nice. Yes, we say. Yes! There's a horsefly attacking, but yes! He leans over the motor, cord in hand, and throws his body into the pull. Once, twice, and the motor sputters to life. He backs the boat into deeper water and comes out to us. Juli hasn't been in the boat yet, so we get her and Lish to climb in by standing on the paddleboard and taking a big step over the railing. The girls zoom off to see the sights. Now, just Alex and I rest in the wake, drifting away from shore with the wind, paddling a bit to get back, then drifting again.

The horsefly attacks once more. We dip and dodge and swing paddles. There's blood on his shoulder. And after more flailing, Alex
stuns the fly with a nice paddle chop. The fly on its back in the
water, floating like us. I drift over and kill it. Peace now, the rise
and fall of each wave, though I feel bad about the fly.

We talk like brothers, comfortable, though we mostly keep saying again and again how nice the water is, how sublime the sun
is, the air, the cloudlessness. There isn't much else to say. What
more could there be? And I feel compelled to keep saying "It's so
beautiful. The water is so good," as if repetition will make what we
have here permanent. Fifteen minutes go by in that state of awe
until the boat echoes across the water. They're still far off, but my
father's voice reaches us all the same. He's telling the girls that you
can't get boats like his anymore and he's got the only one, and it's
such a thing he would tell them, so perfect for the moment, that
we break into uncontrolled laughter. My chest aches with it. Our
father's essence contained in that story, how no one has the same
boat as him, and I wish I could stay there forever, in a slow drift
from shore, hearing that story or other stories, able to know who
someone is without seeing them.

Acknowledgements

THOUGH THIS BOOK CONCERNS PERIODS in my life that often left me feeling isolated, I was anything but during the process of its creation.

First and foremost, my big, hilarious, indelible family has been there for me always, providing care and love and — yes — financial assistance, without which my life would have taken a very different trajectory. My parents, Sue and Jacques, and my siblings, Alex, Angela, and Jessica, are the best people and I'm so lucky to have them. They've sat through treatments and come to the hospital with a change of clothes and a charger for my headphones. They've brought me soup when I was prone in bed, miserable. In fact, many people over the years have brought me soup while I was prone in bed, and you all know who you are and deserve crowns.

My agent, Akin, took a chance on me and my work even as he was just starting an agency, and it took years to get a book out, years where we had to sometimes re-evaluate and go back to the drawing board. His careful eye and artistic drive have been a massive help to my writing and allowed me to reconsider what a book is and can be.

I know these things often include long lists of professors from a writer's alma mater, if they have one, and I'm here to tell you that my list isn't that long. When I first began taking writing classes at the University of Victoria, I was taught by such brilliant professors, many of whom became friends and mentors along the way. The academic writing endeavour is not without flaws, but I truly valued my time there and consider it such a gift. So here goes: First and foremost, I need to thank Bill Gaston. Bill was my advisor during grad school, and he counselled me on how I should approach my thesis while doing chemotherapy; he's taken me into his home and welcomed me like family over the years, and without him this book would certainly not exist. Other faculty and staff at UVic's writing program that I must thank include Lorna Crozier, Lorna Jackson, Joan MacLeod, Steven Price, John Gould, Lee Henderson, Carla Funk, Tim Lilburn, and the inimitable Valerie — all these figures inspired me and were tough on me and gave me a chance.

My editor, Susan Fitzgerald, helped shape this memoir in the small, difficult ways that end up making a big difference. The subtle work of an editor creates the whole and gives a thing unity. Her understanding of the book's goals, of its voice, were clear from the first note of hers that I read. I can't thank her and Dundurn enough for the editorial guidance and work they've put into this project.

I've always been fortunate to be part of such a generous community of writers on Vancouver Island, and they've readily swapped edits and workshopped excerpts from this book and driven me around and provided life advice and been awesome people. To Dave, Annabel, Steph, Susan, K'ari, Erin, and many more, you've been good friends to me.

It must be said that without the support I've received from The Canada Council for the Arts and Andrew Wilkinson with the Tiny Foundation, writing this book would have been much more difficult. Organizations such as these provide such crucial support to artists, even ones that work full-time at a day job, and I can't thank them enough.

Lastly, I must thank Juli, who has been with me through the entire process of writing this book, who got me to read parts to her at night — the real editing — and who has been a beacon in my life since I met her. *Te amo.*

About the Author

Photo by Chelsey Warren

JASON JOBIN WAS BORN AND raised on an acreage outside of Whitehorse, Yukon, in a cabin his father built. After high school, he moved to Victoria, B.C., to study in the University of Victoria's writing program, where he did his B.A. and M.F.A. He lives in Victoria, and when he's not beating cancer, likes to play squash at the university. His non-fiction has been longlisted for the CBC prize, been published in Cleaver magazine, Pithead Chapel, and *The Sun Magazine*. His stories have won a National Magazine Award and been featured in the 2018 and 2019 Writers' Trust McClelland & Stewart Journey Prize anthologies. He's been shortlisted for the Commonwealth Short Story Prize and been a finalist for *American Short Fiction*'s Halifax Ranch Fiction Prize, as well as won the *Malahat Review*'s Jack Hodgins Founders' and Far Horizons awards for fiction. Jason currently has no pets and is allergic to dogs, cats, and horses, but he secretly likes dogs, especially big ones that lean on you when their hips are sore and arthritic — he may be in the market for one.